THE DUST
IN THE BALANCE

THE DUST
IN THE BALANCE

British Women in India 1905–1945

Pat Barr

'Women in all countries are considered such dust in
the balance when their interests are pitted against
those of men.'

Fanny Parks, *Wanderings of a Pilgrim in Search of the Picturesque
Travels in India*, 1850

HAMISH HAMILTON · LONDON

HAMISH HAMILTON LTD

Published by the Penguin Group
27 Wrights Lane, London W8 5TZ, England
Viking Penguin Inc, 40 West 23rd Street, New York, New York 10010, U.S.A.
Penguin Books Australia Ltd, Ringwood, Victoria, Australia
Penguin Books Canada Ltd, 2801 John Street, Markham, Ontario, Canada
L3R 1B4
Penguin Books (N.Z.) Ltd, 182–190 Wairau Road, Auckland 10, New Zealand

Penguin Books Ltd, Registered Offices: Harmondsworth, Middlesex, England

First published in Great Britain 1989 by
Hamish Hamilton Ltd

Copyright © 1989 by Pat Barr

1 3 5 7 9 10 8 6 4 2

British Library Cataloguing in Publication Data
CIP data for this book is available from the British Library

ISBN 0–241–12808–0

Typeset at The Spartan Press Ltd,
Lymington, Hants
Printed in Great Britain by
Butler and Tanner Ltd, Frome, Somerset

For my dear friend,
Mary Mason

Contents

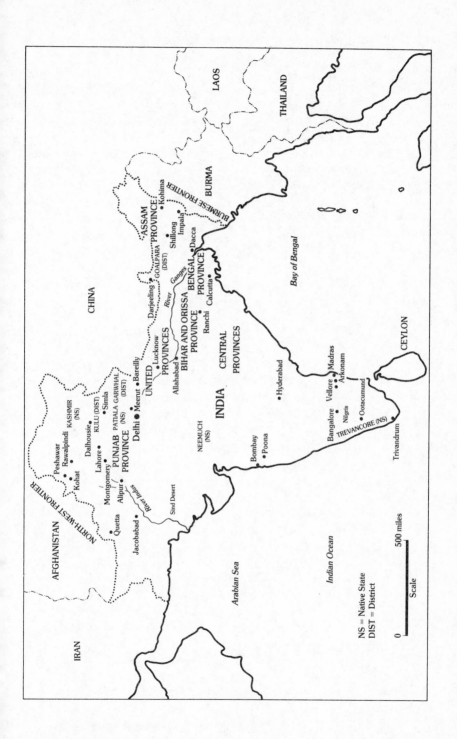

List of Illustrations

A 'purdah picnic' in the hills. (Waterhouse Collection in the Cambridge South Asian Archive)

Margaret Cousins as the first woman magistrate appointed in India. (Ganesh & Co, Madras)

Margaret Cousins. (Ganesh & Co, Madras)

Margaret Ussher during the war. (The British Library – India Office Library & Records)

Lady Linlithgow inspecting a WACI parade in Delhi. (Trustees of the Imperial War Museum)

The WVS prepare a welcome for returning troops. (Trustees of the Imperial War Museum)

American soldiers in Karachi. (Mrs A. Swayne-Thomas)

Serving the troops. (Rumer Godden, from *Bengal Journey*)

Checking the stores. (Rumer Godden, from *Bengal Journey*)

Jacket photographs

The publishers would like to thank the following for permission to reproduce their photographs: The British Library – India Office Library & Records, for the picture of the University Settlement Women Students' Hostel, Bombay; Mrs I. Portal for the picture of her wedding; The Trustees of the Imperial War Museum for Lady Linlithgow inspecting the troops; Rumer Godden for 'serving the troops'; and Mrs O. Hamilton for the picture of her and her husband crossing a river.

Acknowledgements

I would like first of all to express my gratitude to Miss Mary Thatcher, former archivist of the Centre of South Asian Studies in Cambridge, who first suggested the subject of this book to me and whose collection of women's records has proved an invaluable resource. I am similarly grateful to Dr Lionel Carter, Secretary-Librarian of the Centre, who was enthusiastic about the subject from the beginning and also provided me with many useful leads.

Appropriately, Miss Thatcher made her suggestion to me at a meeting of the British Association for Cemeteries in South Asia – an organization which is much livelier than it sounds. I am most grateful to the several members of BACSA who responded to my request for material, and in particular to A. Baylis, B. Macdonald and M. Wright from whose books, published by BACSA, I have quoted. I would also like to thank BACSA's chairman, Michael Stokes, and secretary, Theon Wilkinson, for their unfailing courtesy and help.

I am indebted to the authors of the following privately printed books for permission to quote from them: A. Chitty, D. Coelho and Dr R. Roseveare, and to A. Bolton for the quotations from *The Maturing Sun*, published by Headline Books. It was thanks to Dr Roseveare that I had the privilege of a brief meeting with Miss Marjorie Sykes when she was in England last year.

I would like to express my thanks to all the women whom I met personally. It was a great pleasure to talk to them about their experiences of India and I received much kindness and hospitality from them. I am especially grateful to Mrs Iris Portal who is always willing to offer valuable help on the subject of India.

In the course of my research I also consulted the manuscript collection of the India Office Library and I would like to acknowledge their courtesy in making their materials available to me. Acknowledgement is also made to the BBC in respect of those recordings originally made for their *Plain Tales from the Raj* series and now deposited at the IOL. In this regard, I would also like to thank Mr Charles Allen, author of the book of the series, for his cooperation. I record due acknowledgement to the British in India Oral Archives Committee in respect of the recordings from which I have quoted and which were made under their auspices. I am also indebted to the Imperial War Museum for the manuscript records I consulted.

Lastly, I would like to express grateful thanks to several people who sent me unpublished memoirs or letters and to all the women quoted in this book who considered it worthwhile to put on record, in some form or other, the stories of their lives in India.

Pat Barr
May 1989

Chronological Events

1911	Delhi Durbar. Delhi proclaimed future capital.
1916–21	**Viceroy: Lord Chelmsford.**
1918	Montagu-Chelmsford Report. Proposals for increasing Indian participation in administration.
1919	Government of India Act. Introduction of constitutional steps towards self-government.
1921–26	**Viceroy: Lord Reading.**
1926–30	**Viceroy: Lord Irwin.**
1928	Simon Commission to review earlier reforms.
1931–35	**Viceroy: Lord Willingdon.**
1931	Inauguration of New Delhi.
1935	Government of India Act. Further constitutional advances towards Dominion status for India.
1936–43	**Viceroy: Lord Linlithgow.**
1939	Second world war begins.
1942	Fall of Singapore. Japanese invasion of Burma.
1943–46	**Viceroy: Lord Wavell.**
1944	Japanese offensive into Assam. Battles of Imphal and Kohima.
1945	End of second world war. Surrender of Japanese.

Introduction

In my earlier book about British women of the Victorian age in India*, I suggested that the popular stereotype of the idle, frivolous, snobbish, selfish 'memsahib' was less than a half-truth 'built on historical clichés of little substance.' The stereotype is even less true of those twentieth-century women in India who feature most prominently in this story. But it still persists, even though the range and length of their Indian experience was usually greater than that of their forebears and many of them were engaged in some kind of professional or voluntary work.

The persistence of the memsahib stereotype is due, first, to the long-standing, built-in masculine bias of historical studies, which has meant that women's contributions generally have remained undervalued and usually unpublished. Secondly, it is unfortunate that, though there are a growing number of female historians trying to redress the balance, most seem to have a built-in political bias, on this particular subject, against all forms of 'colonialism'. It is my contention, however, that the lives of British women in twentieth-century India are as valid and of as much consequence in our female history as those of, say, the working girls of our industrial northern cities.

It is characteristic of women's subordinate standing in 'our island story' that, last year, it was suggested I should abandon this project because a book on a similar theme appeared†, even though it covered the entire span of the

*_The Memsahibs_, Secker & Warburg, 1976.
†_Women of the Raj_, Margaret Macmillan, 1988.

British female presence in India. Hundreds if not thousands of books about the lives and work of British men in
India have been published and more undoubtedly will be.
There is, as a result, a general awareness that men's
experience of the country differed very greatly according to
region, actual years of residence, type of work, hierarchical
position – not to mention the constant variable of individual temperament. Obviously these same differences
affected their wives, whose surroundings and life styles
were largely defined by their husbands' work and status –
though their reactions to circumstance were equally individual. The experiences of British women who pursued their
own careers in India were subject to the same variations as
those of their male compatriots.

My first aim, therefore, has been to show just how
diverse, extraordinary and far-flung women's experiences
were and how many of them had often to contend with
measures of discomfort, isolation and risk that were far
removed from the red-carpeted luxury of popular imagina-
tion. In pursuit of this aim, I have drawn almost entirely
on unpublished or little-known material rather than on
the familiar works of professional writers and prominent
personalities. Numerous British women would qualify for
inclusion in this book, but I could do no more than focus on
relatively few individuals who have selected themselves,
as it were, either by writing especially vivid, original
accounts that have reached one of the public archives,
by responding to my requests for material, or by
giving interesting oral interviews either to me or to other
researchers.

Some of the memorialists were outstanding in their
particular fields; others describe with particular cogency
the kinds of experiences, endeavours, pleasures and tribul-
ations that were shared by many. My selection has had to
be somewhat random and idiosyncratic and I do not claim
to have made a comprehensive historical survey of the
subject. I regret a certain inevitable imbalance in the social

distribution of the contributors – as is usually the case with books of this type. It was still an age when the Colonel's Lady and the Viceroy's Wife received every encouragement to chronicle their lives for posterity, while those of the rank and file were seldom considered worthy of record – even by themselves.

It was also an age in which the modern trend to 'tell it all exactly as it was' was not fashionable; and one must remember, in any case, that people invariably tailor their memories of the past to suit the shibboleths of the present. So, for instance, I suspect that the amount of racialism current in the ordinary social circles of British India has been played down in retrospect. In retrospect too, several wives seem quite defensive about their lives in India, which may well be due both to the extreme anti-colonialism of the immediate post-war era and to the growth of feminism that has emphasized women's responsibility to develop their talents and initiatives in their own right.

However, the ordered structures of authority and power which the British had created in India by the twentieth century allowed little room for unconventional ambitions or untoward behaviour of that or any other kind. Their dominion was divided into three presidencies (Bombay, Bengal, Madras) and seven provinces, with the Viceroy at the apex of authority. Governors of the presidencies were usually distinguished men who came out from England while the provinces were usually ruled by senior men in the Indian Civil Service. Each province was divided into a number of districts under the administration of a District Officer whose job it was to deal with matters of justice and revenue.

Social status within the ICS was awarded strictly in relation to a man's position and the same status was automatically conferred upon his wife. Similar levels of precedence existed in the army, the judiciary, the services of education and health, the railways. The entire class hierarchy was carefully codified in a guide – indispensable to any social climber – entitled the *Warrant of Precedence*, which gave precise information on the exact amount of deference due on every formal or social occasion to every man who held an official position (and to his wife).

The entire Indian continent was not governed directly by the British and their precious *Warrant of Precedence* of course. Almost a third of the country remained in the hands of Indian princes or chiefs; these were generally known as the 'Native States' and their inhabitants were not British subjects. By 1935 there was a total of 562 of these states, the comparative importance of each being defined by the number of gun salutes its ruler merited on ceremonial occasions. The states varied greatly in size and splendour and to each was allotted a British Resident or Agent whose function was to liaise between its rulers and the Government of India.

The impetus towards changing this essentially static state of affairs, which allowed Indians very little say in the government of their own country, gained strength after the first world war and sporadically disrupted the status quo during the 1920s and 1930s. Western-educated Indians became increasingly resentful of their exclusion from the superior ranks of the administrative services and the Indian Congress became increasingly militant. The charismatic Indian leaders, Mahatma Gandhi and Jawaharlal Nehru, initiated various popular demonstrations and political campaigns to further the goal of self-government which resulted in the spread of anti-British, pro-nationalist fervour to many parts of the country.

The process of slow, often reluctant constitutional advance towards Indian independence was interrupted by the outbreak of the second world war. In the course of it, two and a half million Indians volunteered to fight on the Allied side – and Britain faced increasing pressures from various quarters to 'Quit India'. Two years after the war's end it did so.

This, then, was the historical context that framed the lives of the British women who are featured here. Its factual outlines may be fairly familiar, but its prevailing moral and social climate seems strange and distant to us nowadays. Take, for instance, the degree of straightforward, unquestioning patriotism, with its concomitant ideal of service to an empire which, it was commonly believed, was endowed with certain intrinsic qualities of moral, cultural and religious superiority – not to mention a near monopoly of political wisdom. These attitudes have been so discredited as to seem rather sinister and utterly absurd today. Yet they were shared (with varying degrees of certainty) by most British who lived in India at the time. Such beliefs provided both inspiration and justification for their ruling presence and sanction for the fact that they discounted, even denigrated, India's struggle towards independence.

The imperial scenario, with its confident aura of public grandeur and paternalistic authority, which was based on these convictions, was created by British men, with only a few subordinate roles allotted to their womenfolk. During the first decades of the century the nature of these roles changed little from those of their Victorian mothers and grandmothers – many of whom had also had experience of India, for the country ran in families. Young women of the middle classes, who formed the bulk of the 'memsahib' population, led sheltered childhoods and received conventional schooling intended to fit them for their secondary parts. While boys were trained to think of themselves as leaders and pillars of authority, girls were expected only to support, to follow, to help maintain 'proper standards' that accentuated the distances between rulers and ruled.

Once settled in India, the women seldom questioned these tenets partly because they were not expected to question anything. Protected and excluded from the actual business of ruling, they generally made the best of things as they were. However, improved educational opportunities for women at Home and the scarcity of men after the first world war meant that, from the late 1920s onwards, a growing number of single women went out to work in India in professional capacities. As some of them testify here, their presence was rather unsettling, they suffered from prejudice and lack of status and – as part outsiders – they observed with some astringency the narrow conservatism of the average British-in-India community.

Despite this, all white women in India could not but compare their own lives with those of Indian women – and realize that they were relatively free of constraint, relatively well-educated, relatively healthy. Such comparisons encouraged them 'to count their blessings' (which was perhaps no bad thing) and, in some cases, to try and alleviate the suffering and oppression of the purdah system. The system has often been cited as a principal reason for the lack of real communication between the races. This was certainly true because very few Indian women were allowed to converse freely with foreigners while Indian men were usually inhibited and embarrassed by the presence of British women at official and social functions.

However, a growing awareness of the greater freedoms enjoyed by Western women resulted in a gradual relaxation of purdah restrictions in some quarters which encouraged more social intercourse between them and Indian women – as some of these memoirs suggest. A few British women of radical persuasion were actively engaged in anti-purdah campaigns and the Freedom for India Movement, and their memoirs provide interesting evidence that such non-conformity was just possible, even though, in one case, it led to a jail sentence handed out by the British authorities!

Another kind of freedom from conformity that some British women enjoyed was the chance to accompany their husbands to remote regions blissfully distanced from the watchful eyes of superiors and the petty hierarchies of 'the station'. Many more than I have actually quoted recall with pleasure and nostalgia their nomadic lives in the 'jungle' wilds where they learned to cope with the harsh realities of rural life – and the occasional hair-raising adventure. Many women teachers, missionaries, doctors and nurses spent years working in towns and villages equally far removed from the wider social circles of their compatriots. That very isolation often enabled them to pursue their appointed tasks more independently and extensively than women of their kind were generally permitted to at Home. Incidentally, the work of professional British women in the Indian hinterlands has not received much attention from historians, and I should point out that what appears here is but a brief summary of their considerable achievements.

It is clear from the records that even the lifelong career of the fully-committed professional woman did not rate very highly in the hierarchies of British India. She, and all the other women from Vicereine to soldier's wife, were ultimately answerable and subject to some kind of male authority that created the balances in which their interests weighed but lightly – as Fanny Parks suggests. Some of the women featured here did not notice the imbalance, others noticed but did not mind; a few minded, but could do little about it. Whatever their feelings on this subject, they generally made the best of their lives in India, they rose to many and various occasions, they enjoyed themselves, they put up with quite a lot – and they all have their individual ways of telling us about it.

I

Something Worthwhile

'Our aim was still the same. We were trying to train the girls to think – and give them something worthwhile to think about.'

Miss Florence M. Wyld

On an October day in 1909, Miss Florence Wyld, a thirty-one-year-old clergyman's daughter, walked into the largest room of a house perched on a small hill known as Mount Charles in Hyderabad. She'd been appointed principal of a school for high-caste girls in the city and she was accompanied by three young junior teachers. All of them had just arrived from England and had no prior experience of India. She'd been led to believe that the school was a going concern, but could find no records of former pupils, no timetables, not even a sheet of paper. And this main 'schoolroom' was empty except for a few desks and a cupboard containing six tattered *Royal Readers*. 'One glance was enough to suggest that the best place for them would be the bonfire,' she decided crisply.

However, as she had brought some educational supplies with her, she managed to open the school soon afterwards, but only four pupils came – one for each teacher. The little girls were in strict purdah and eight-foot-high corrugated-iron screens had been erected at a side entrance so that the male servants who drove their carriages could go and hide behind the screens while the pupils dismounted and scurried inside. They were accompanied by their ayahs who carried their books and pencils and at first insisted on settling on the floor beside their desks until Miss Wyld persuaded them to wait in a room below. Lessons started at

9

nine in the morning but purdah quarters did not live by the clock and pupils arrived when 'someone had thought about school'. And although the children were all under ten years old, there were no playing spaces available, and no lavatories either. When Miss Wyld inquired about the latter, she was told that, 'as the zenana school is a day school, it is not understood why these are needed'. Much more essential was the provision of a separate matted room for twice daily prayers and readings from the Koran.

Though the majority of Hyderabad's population was Hindu, the state was run by Moslem government officials, most of whom were opposed to the school's very existence. Weary months of wrangling ensued, therefore, before it was considered a socially acceptable institution and the number of pupils began gradually to increase. Florence was helped through these early difficulties by Khujista Begum, a member of the royal family who 'had wonderful foresight, vision and ambition for Indian girls'. With these sentiments Florence was naturally in sympathy. She had seen her family's money spent on her six brothers' education not on her own, and, though she'd eventually managed to get herself to Oxford, no degree was awarded to her because she was a woman. She'd taught at St Paul's school in London, and, not surprisingly, had been active in the suffrage movement.

In Hyderabad, as at Home, Miss Wyld had to fight on several fronts, for she and her colleagues found themselves virtually confined within a rambling old bungalow next to the school compound. On grounds of purdah propriety, no men other than their servants were to be allowed into the bungalow, Miss Wyld was told – a rule she eventually circumvented by having a high wall built between it and the school, so that any 'goings on' were at least unobserved by the pupils! In fact, very little 'went on' for the teachers' social life wasn't exactly exciting.

Their nearest compatriots lived twelve miles away in the army cantonments at Secunderabad and they were provided only with a 'very dilapidated Victoria and a seedy horse' for transport. Members of its Club were friendly on the whole, but Florence discovered (as did many single professional women of her time) that 'the whole social fabric was based on the accepted fact that all women would have a man attached'. In consequence, though she had a university Blue for tennis, she was seldom asked to play in mixed doubles, while 'ladies' fours were unheard of'. The social atmosphere was, she comments, 'rather like a hundred years ago in England'.

In the school, called the Mahbubia after Mahbub, the old Nizam of Hyderabad, things began slowly to improve. The girls agreed to carry their own books and pencils, they studied English, learning words like 'bridge' and 'forest' to describe things they'd never seen. 'We had to be so very graphic,' Florence explained. She armed herself with a globe to give them some idea of the scale of the world beyond their purdah confines and kept asking questions – Why? When? What? – 'and trying to get them to think out answers'. She also 'introduced them to the joy of games by encouraging them to bat a shuttlecock back and forth over a blackboard'.

With quiet persistence she set about breaking down the rigidities of the purdah system. Determined that both the girls and their parents should take this educational experiment seriously, she arranged a system of graded examinations. Two pupils studied the piano but, when it came to their first exam, their fathers decreed they must wear gloves and the concealing *bourkha* because the examiner was a man. Somehow Miss Wyld managed to 'work round' this ruling, and the candidates (able to touch the keys and read the score properly) both passed. Having acquired more educational material from England, she set her older pupils to study for the Cambridge Locals. Although she wanted them to learn Indian history, she couldn't find any English textbooks on the subject, and British history, she suddenly realized, 'took a lot of

explaining'. 'What a lot of wars and quarrels and persecu-
tions there seemed to have been in the name of the
Christian religion', she comments. At Home, she'd taught
history without a qualm and not until then 'had I so
strongly wanted to leave out so much!'

The girls responded with enthusiastic dedication to
every challenge, and within a few years three had passed
their first exams. However, a very promising Moslem
pupil was suddenly whipped away at the age of fourteen to
be married, which made Miss Wyld extremely angry,
especially as the girl's father had been partly educated in
England. Reluctantly, sadly, she attended the wedding.
'But the little bird, the happy child I'd known for several
years, was taking no part in the excitement. She sat on a
couch, dressed in beautiful clothes, but quite still, looking
down all the time.' When Florence spoke to her, she
wouldn't look up or answer.

To escape the occasional discouragements and frustra-
tions of her job, Miss Wyld bought herself a car from an
army officer in Secunderabad. It was an open two-seater
Adams, 'with one cylinder, no gears, pedals to push and a
handle at the side for winding up the engine'. She hired a
small boy to do the winding and eventually '. . . something roared and the boy fell backwards and I pushed the
pedal and shot into the opposite wall'. It took her a while
to get out of that, for the officer had omitted to tell her how
to reverse. But, nothing daunted, Florence and a colleague
set off for the southern hill station of Ootacumund on their
next holiday.

'Recollect that no native whatever is capable of judging
distances or speeds', wrote one Mrs Lloyd, author of *India
for the Motorist*, published in 1913. Therefore it was 'always
needful to sound the horn frequently and well at long
distances if the car wishes to clear a passage. Ordinary
pedestrians often show an astonishing disregard for the
presence of a car and will not move till the very last
moment.' So, sounding the horn, overtaking bullock carts,

just avoiding amazed and immobilized pedestrians, the two teachers reached the foothills below Ooty. Gamely the Adams chugged 8000 feet upwards, with great bursts of steam shooting at intervals from its radiator into the air. 'We literally boiled our way up the ghat' – having nervously backed and doubled round each hairpin bend. Their eventual arrival caused a gratifying stir among the hill-station residents, though Miss Wyld was a little chagrined to learn from the garage man that the car did possess a bottom gear after all – which would have made things easier.

Back in Hyderabad, 'Miss Ma', as the pupils called Florence, again took up her task of encouraging in her pupils 'a sense of confidence of the innate value of each individual and their powers of thought and reason'. One problem was to increase their numbers; new recruits aged between six and nine years might come at any time – and sometimes disappear with equal unpredictability. It was quite a triumph when a positive cavalcade suddenly appeared in the compound one day. 'A very large carriage was preceded by two outriders in special livery, two more outriders bringing up the rear.' From the carriage emerged 'three beautifully dressed girls . . . decked in precious jewellery'. They were the daughters of one of the city's chief nobles, and greatly enhanced the school's prestige, though at first Miss Wyld had difficulty in persuading their ayahs to remove all that jewellery during lessons.

When the school roll reached forty, the first prize-giving was held and, as there could be no music or sports to entertain the parents, the girls acted scenes from *A Midsummer Night's Dream*, 'with lots of fairies in pretty saris'. As the school grew in size and reputation so did its pupils' ambitions, and by 1918 a few begged to enter for the Senior Cambridge examinations. So Miss Wyld found herself having to teach physical geography, which she'd not studied herself before, to girls whose first-hand experience of the earth's surface was confined within the purdah-imposed boundaries of the city.

Teachers and pupils worked hard for two years, but when the exam papers arrived Miss Wyld was dismayed to see questions about the construction of a railway on an up gradient – none of the examinees having ever seen a train or a line. Nevertheless all the girls who took the exam passed and, in a memoir written when she was in her nineties and blind, Florence Wyld allowed herself justifiable pride at that. 'It was', she wrote, 'our first real milestone.' Looking back on the day when she first walked into the one schoolroom with its few desks and its four pupils, she recorded that, when she resigned due to ill-health in 1919, one hundred students were on the school roll and six of them had passed Cambridge Senior examinations.

As Hyderabad was a Native State, the British had no jurisdiction over its educational system, which was why Miss Wyld had to do battle against those Moslem officials who thought that girls' education was not only a waste of money but downright dangerous because it bred discontent and insubordination among them. In British India, however, a network of primary schools existed by the early twentieth century, though it was not comprehensive and varied greatly in standard. Because many Indian parents shared the views of the Moslem officials, girl pupils were very much in a minority and female literacy rates were low.

Nevertheless, in 1908, the India Office appointed Miss H.G. Stuart as 'Chief Inspectress' of girls' schools in the Upper Provinces. Aided by a staff of mainly Eurasian 'sub-inspectresses', her job was to report on conditions in schools run by the government, by district or municipal boards or by missionary societies. Girls began school about six years old and left about ten, 'mainly with a view to improving their marriage prospects'. Their parents felt it was important that each child should receive a doll at every prize-giving – which could later be shown off 'as proof of having been so many years in school'. Few of them paid fees and some were bribed to let their children attend. All in all, an inspectress's job was 'rather a queer life', Miss Stuart soon decided. 'Touring up and down in uncomfortable places for about half a year and eating queer meals on trains. Not very exciting or romantic in fact.'

Several years later Miss Stuart was joined by an assistant who had the excitement and romance of India in her blood. Her name was Alice Lawrence, a member of the famous Lawrence family who'd served in India for generations. She was also possessed of a keen eye, a quick wit and a modern outlook which, in 1922, quite frightened her superiors. The men of the Education Department here 'are awfully behind the times' she soon decided. 'My appearance gave them rather a shock and they can't grasp how someone who ought to be a blue stocking can look rather like a butterfly.' Their womenfolk, also disconcerted by her youthful good looks, determined to guard her carefully. 'It's rather funny to be chaperoned by an entire Department,' she wrote to her mother.

Miss Lawrence's first resolve was to learn the ropes from Miss Stuart ('a delightful person, nice and unconventional and full of go') so she could 'snap my fingers at the Victorianism of the Education Department'. Certainly she was a match for them. When one official queried 'the fitness of women for administrative posts because they're apt to fuss over their work and wear themselves out', Miss Lawrence riposted that, as women are older for their age than men, they ought, on the contrary, to get administrative posts when younger.

Leaving the officials to fret, she soon set off with Miss Stuart on her tours of inspection. They travelled hundreds of miles by train, staying in Circuit Houses and PWD bungalows, '. . . never quite knowing where we'll end up next. However Miss Stuart and I are both very calm and take it as it comes.' What came was an exhausting succession of schools that all seemed very odd to Alice Lawrence. Some teachers were 'very ignorant of everything beyond the basics of reading and arithmetic' and had a 'curiously casual' approach to education generally. Often, the schools had no set timetables so that it was difficult for even the most diligent inspectresses to organize schemes of work for them, and problems of religion, caste and custom arose when communal examinations were proposed. Some pupils were already married, for instance, and permission had to be obtained from parents and husbands before they could face a male examiner.

Government-run schools were supposed to be free of religious instruction, but this was hard to enforce. Miss Stuart once came upon a teacher who'd written a large 'O' and 'M' at the top of the board. 'O', she explained, represented an infinite circle and 'M' an infinite sound that might go on forever. The inspectress decided not to interfere. The overtly Christian mission schools took in all who could be persuaded to attend them – even sweepers' children, 'jolly little people making a clay house and furnishing it with clay utensils and listening to stories'. But in general mission schools lacked jollity, Miss Lawrence felt. 'It's curious how unattractive missionaries manage to make them . . . All the quaintness and picturesqueness done away with, and the clothes of both staff and girls so ugly. And there's a sort of barrack and institutional atmosphere about them.'

Though Miss Lawrence didn't much like the mission schools, she also disapproved of some Indian teachers' methods. She once heard a child ask why the moon was called a 'she'. The teacher explained it was because the sun was higher and brighter than the moon, and to reinforce the point, he made the whole class chant, 'The sun is bright; he is a man. The moon is not bright; she is a woman'. The young inspectress naturally objected to that, for she was indubitably 'bright' – and also pretty. One of the Education Department wives forecast, 'We won't have her for long. She's much too pretty.' In that she was correct; in less than two years Miss Lawrence left to marry a Mr Stokes to whom many of the letters about her job had been addressed. And Miss Stuart commented later with slightly bitter perception that, given her background, Alice had felt she ought to work in India. 'But I don't think she found she could bear it . . . I think she rather hurried that marriage so as to depart and keep a good face.'

Miss Stuart attended the wedding, remained single, returned to the unromantic rounds of a chief inspectress.

For the great majority of the British in India, of course, education centred on the provision of a thoroughly English schooling for one's offspring.

Heart-rending tales abound of parents' sadness at parting with children and the latter's sorrow at leaving India, their sense of exile in what was always called Home. Edith Dixon, whose father was a railway superintendent before the First War, was sent Home to school aged seven – which was quite usual. The preparations frightened her. 'Father painted my name very beautifully in white on a black tin trunk', and then took her to Calcutta where she went on board ship. 'And I can remember standing at the rail surrounded by families and watching my father waving on the dock-side and gradually disappear.' But in England 'everything was wrong'. Her clothes were the wrong colours and 'a joke at school because they were behind the times'. And she 'used to hear people say, "Oh how beautiful the moors are!" And I used to think to myself – I don't know what beautiful is. Nothing's beautiful here, and I didn't think so. It took me a long time to see that England was beautiful – it was too tame.' England was colourless, small, dull; India was vibrant, warm, exciting.

To keep that vibrant memory alive Betsy Macdonald's mother sent little parcels to her at her English boarding school. 'These either had scented sandalwood boxes or little figures of animals made of wood or papier-mâché. Indian bangles of all kinds, the ones I loved best being of coloured glass like satin ribbons, and in one box was a bright silken sari so fine it could be pulled through a wedding ring. Much as I loved receiving these, it made me very homesick for mother and India, which I still thought of as home – even the thick white cloth she sewed the parcels in smelt of the country.'

Despite the sense of exile, most children accepted it as inevitable, even as natural because it was a recurring pattern of British life in India. Mrs Ravenscroft, whose great-grandfather was with the East India Company in 1802, whose grandfather was in the Mutiny, remembers the actual time of separation from parents as 'terrible when it was happening, but like children you sort of forgot after a while . . . I suppose we just thought that was the way life was, and when we came across children who expressed astonishment at your mother being in one country and you in another, you were just as bewildered as they were and thought how very odd they don't live as we live'.

Boys, whose education was considered more important, nearly always suffered the ordeals of English boarding-school life from seven onwards, but girls were sometimes taught by governesses and/or sent to hill-station schools if they were 'delicate' or family finances were limited. The latter still meant living away from one's family for the long school term between March and November, a period which, as Denise Coelho wrote, seemed absolutely interminable. During the first week of March for seven consecutive years she left Calcutta for the Dow Hill School near Darjeeling equipped much as her peers in England with name-tapes written in Stephen's indelible ink, navy serge bloomers, the inevitable black tin trunk. To it, however, was strapped a canvas bedroll for the overnight train which left Sealdah station at nine in the evening. 'Everyone was leaning out of the windows, waving white handkerchiefs kept at the ready for this moment . . . Athletic fathers were much admired for their ability to run alongside their daughters' compartments touching hands for as long as possible. Suddenly the train began to gather speed and they ran out of platform. We moved into the vast Indian night, glimpsing dimly lit and distant locomotive sheds and the hurricane lanterns of coolie gangs working late beside other sets of railway lines . . . Another nine months of boarding school had begun.'

Dow Hill School had been opened in Victorian times and, like others of its kind, its curriculum was fashioned entirely on the Home model, about the only concessions to its actual location being that its 'houses' were named after three governor-generals of India and that its pupils wore solar-topees instead of straw panamas. There were other extra-curricular differences however. From the dormitory windows the girls enjoyed spectacular views of the snowy ranges of the Himalayas and in the surrounding forests wild epiphytic orchids 'grew on the mossy banks bordering our walks. We cultivated them in Peak Frean biscuit tins bedded down on bark covered with furry moss torn from the hillsides and they flourished on the window-sills of our classrooms. On a warm summer day the air was filled with their cloyingly sweet perfume.' Other, less attractive denizens of the forests were black leeches that fastened on the girls' legs and 'on school picnics we carried little packets of salt so we could sprinkle it on the leeches and watch them shrivel and fall off'.

Apart from walks and picnics there weren't many treats except an occasional visit to Darjeeling's cinema, listening to popular tunes on a friend's wind-up gramophone and the Saturday tuck. This they bought from Guru Mea, 'a dapper little Nepalese' who wore white jodhpur-style trousers with a European jacket and a small forage cap and spread out his wares (Sharp's toffees, peppermint rock) on the steps of the old library. There wasn't much else to do at weekends except loll about the hillsides, chatting, reading and watching the local Pahari children. They were most appealing, with 'pale round faces, Mongolian features, black hair and large, lustrous eyes. Throughout the year they roamed the hillsides barefoot and agile as the mountain goats they sometimes herded.' The girls, in their neat school uniforms watched the undernourished little Pahari boys 'ski' on one leg down a steep tiled drain in the hillside on knuckle bones grasped by the toes or toss marigold flowerheads into the air 'using the inside of one bare foot'.

Despite these brighter moments, Denise, like most of the girls, felt exiled in the forests and mountains and counted the days to the long 'cold-weather hols'. When the magic November day came, they ran and sang towards the station, throwing their topees in the air and watching them roll downhill. At the station they found the delicious Darjeeling oranges, 'packed in hessian-lined local baskets', costing but one rupee a hundred, that they'd ordered as presents for their families. At Siliguri, where they left the toy-sized train of the Darjeeling-Himalayan railway, India surrounded them again with the vendors' familiar cries of: 'Paan, biri cigarettes and gurrum gurrum char'. Joyously the girls settled in the broad-gauge train and the seniors rose early in the morning 'to tie a Homeward Bound placard on the front of the engine at Ranaghat!'

Girls who didn't go away to school anywhere suffered no pangs of exile and their British-in-India childhood is remembered, in retrospect at least, as totally secure and golden. The standard of education they received varied, of course, and few were taught much relating to India except for Rudyard Kipling's children's stories. Some parents joined the Parents' National Education Union which sent out textbooks and instruction courses based on English curricula. Monica Clough, who grew up on a tea estate in Trevancore, remembers being enrolled when she was five and receiving a badge of a dove encircled 'with the cryptic motto: "I am, I can, I ought, I will"'. The courses were thorough but old-fashioned with 'rather tedious text-books' such as *Parables from Nature* in which one Mrs Gatty 'drew a moral from the industrious ant and the winter-sleeping hedgehog'.

Like Monica's mother, the parents of Audrey Baylis (née Clay) took the education of their children seriously. She and her sister spent six 'golden' years in the remote district of Garhwal, where their father, Joseph Clay, was appointed Deputy Commissioner in 1913. Their bunga-low stood in a large compound overlooking the town of Pauri and on a mountain slope where 'everything faced Tibet'. The Clays had acquired the services of Miss Gladys Stewart to help with the children's upbringing and, as Audrey describes it, she received *her* first lesson on arrival at the railhead where she learned how to mount Lakshmi, the Commissioner's elephant.

At a signal 'Lakshmi went quietly down on her knees and remained gently blowing into the dust with her trunk while someone held her tail to form a second step against her side in a loop above her ankle – it being the first step. Gladys had to take firm hold of the rope that passed from Lakshmi's throat, over the pad and under her tail like a crupper, and haul herself up; sometimes quite a difficult scramble'. When Mother and the two children were also aboard, Lakshmi got up very slowly and set off at a steady rolling gait, 'her big round feet going plop plop in the powdery white dust'.

Once settled in the bungalow, Daisy Clay arranged a very comprehensive schedule of home instruction for her daughters. A usual day began 'with fifteen minutes dril-ling using Indian clubs and dumb-bells and lots of deep-breathing exercises'. Then came nursery breakfast with

Gladys and along to the dining-room by nine o'clock for lessons on a big solid table covered with its 'Victorian cloth of green plush and its fringe of wool bobbles'. Text books were acquired from Thacker Spinks of Calcutta: nature study – 'how to grow beans in water etc'; history from *Round the World Tales of Travel*; multiplication tables from Longman's arithmetic series. Sometimes, for encouragement, Joseph presented one or other of them with a book prize for good work or good conduct.

At midday they had a break and a romp with Ruganath Singh, their favourite *chaprassi*, a fair-skinned hill-brahmin. 'Like all Indian servants he was wonderful at playing with children. He would pretend to be a bear or tiger and charge them, or to be a horse with one of them riding piggy-back, the other rushing about like a dog.' Afternoons were for writing 'proper' letters Home to Granny, sewing, including button-holing and embroidery, and learning poetry for later recitation to visitors, such as 'The Wreck of the Steamship Puffin'.

Gladys taught them music-hall songs and hymns for Sunday 'church-going'. There being no actual church for many miles round, Joseph Clay took over, 'like the Captain of his ship, making it a rule to celebrate Matins in the drawing-room round about eleven o'clock'. After a usually rather ragged start, the four-strong congregation followed the Order of Service, 'making the Responses to the Prayers read by Joseph', and concluding with a hymn, sung unaccompanied with Gladys in the lead.

Gladys Stewart remained on good terms with the Clay family during the six years they spent together with little respite from each other's company, but things didn't always work so smoothly. Qualified governesses and children's nurses of the 1920s and 1930s had rather a bad reputation for sailing off to India at their future employers' expense, getting involved in a shipboard romance and marrying as soon as they landed. But, in places where the social scene was both livelier and more structured

than at Garhwal, those who remained single still posed
certain problems. They were definitely superior to the
Indian servants, but were not on a social par with their
employers either. Governesses might eat lunch with the
family including the children, but wouldn't be expected to
dress for dinner and were often served supper by themselves on a tray. They were seldom invited to dances and,
if they could join the Club, it was 'usually on the same
monthly basis as the hospital nurses'. Worried by the
ambiguities of all this, one wife confessed to her former
governess years later that she habitually arranged dinner
parties to coincide with her night off.

Though the situation had its drawbacks, it was one of the
few ways for a single woman of spirit, independence and
'respectability' to see the world – which some of them
certainly did and, in Muriel Le Mesurier's words, 'had an
absolutely fizzing time of it'. Born and brought up in the
Orkneys, Muriel Flaas (as she then was) went to
Aberdeen University and took a teachers' training course
because her mother was determined she should be able to
earn her own living. 'I didn't really want to teach, but I
did want to travel', she explained, and so applied to the
Governesses' Benevolent Institute in London for a job.
    That was in the 1920s, though the institute was still
somewhat Victorian in outlook and had earlier been run
as an Asylum for Decayed Governesses to retire into. But
it had a sound reputation, and 'aristocrats and others of
the better class' applied to it for ladies well qualified to
instruct their offspring – often when they were posted
overseas. In this fashion, Muriel Le Mesurier had already
travelled to Austria, China and America ('and had got
engaged to somebody as usual in each place but didn't
follow through') before, in 1937, she escorted to India the
three older daughters of Sir Roger Lumley who'd been
appointed Governor of Bombay.
    The Lumleys had gone on ahead, leaving her to sort out

the problems of getting the children, a staff that included a nanny, a housekeeper and a maid, together with 'at least forty large packing cases' from Lumley Castle to Tilbury in time for embarkation. She hired buses to cope with it all and while in London 'bought lots of second-hand textbooks from Foyles because no-one else had thought about it.' She even tried to get a simple textbook on Indian history, 'but, you know, there wasn't a single one available'.

At this superior level of the British-in-India hierarchy a place was prepared for everyone and everyone knew it, so there was no agonizing over the niceties of correct behaviour towards a single governess. The gubernatorial establishment at Bombay consisted of a number of very superior bungalows standing in spacious and beautiful grounds. The largest was the Royal Bungalow 'presided over by a self-important major domo with a very grand turban' which contained a ballroom and a dining-room that could seat a hundred. Their Excellencies occupied an imposing two-storey dwelling and there were clusters of bungalows for ADCs, for military personnel and private secretaries.

Miss Flaas and her charges were allotted the Point Bungalow, detached from the rest on a small promontory and with a wide verandah overlooking a private beach, 'which was a lovely spot for a quiet swim'. She went riding with the girls early in the morning (each accompanied by a bodyguard) and then they settled down to work in a schoolroom 'which was just a sitting-room with a round table in it'. She was very keen for the girls to receive a proper education and insisted that the eldest study for her Junior Cambridge. 'I was always having arguments with parents over that one. Their attitude was, Why bother? Our daughters will make good marriages anyway. But I used to say, "There might be a revolution one day and they'll have to earn their own living!" The idea horrified people of that class – but I was right in a way, as things turned out.'

The education of the Lumley girls was scarcely a full-time occupation, but their governess's duties didn't end there. 'I was always being called upon to "make up the numbers" at luncheon, tea and dinner parties. Not qualifying for a top table, she 'often found myself next to an Indian who was nibbling on a bit of lettuce and saying nothing'. As a member of the permanent House Party one was 'always on parade as it were. We had to wear formal dress every evening and hats and gloves even to go to the beach hut at Juhu because we drove in government cars.' Still, it was great fun most of the time, though Miss Flaas sometimes yearned for a night off from 'all that polite chat about nothing much. Of course, I never enjoyed throwing my weight about – like Nanny did.'

Nanny, though not one of the House Party, certainly nurtured aspirations of grandeur. She'd set her tone from the first by demanding her own stateroom on the voyage out and, at garden parties, liked to stand on her verandah and 'wave to the guests with a sort of royal salute'. When Their Excellencies were away on tour, she organized grand dinner parties for the 'bandy boys and their wives' – when the best wines were served and the most expensive cigars smoked!

Women who held positions in the grand households of the Raj remained on the fringes of their employers' social lives; those employed by the Indian aristocracy had more opportunities to mix with Indians as well as their compatriots. Between 1936 and 1943, Miss Margaret Ussher was governess to the three sons of the Begum Sahiba who were wards of the Nizam of Hyderabad. The letters she wrote home to her parents describe a fairly hectic social round, what with dance parties at the Secunderabad Club, visits to the cinema with her charges and ten-course luncheons with visiting maharajahs. She also, incidentally, attended Sports Day at the now-famous Mahbubia School where the students played tennis, netball and hockey – a considerable advance on batting a shuttlecock over a blackboard.

She has little to say about what she taught the boys, but apparently their mother, the Begum, and the Nizam quarrelled constantly and furiously over whether they should receive higher education in India or England. The boys' clothes were a matter of great concern, however, and at the start of each term Miss Ussher interviewed several tailors who made all their outfits, including smart new lounge suits for the Nizam's birthday celebrations and long silk Indian coats for formal dinners.

Sometimes Miss Ussher nicely captures the cloistered, wealthy atmosphere of the aristocratic city families among whom she lived. On the anniversary of the death of the children's grandfather, she accompanied them and their mother to pay their respects. 'We sat in the back of the Silver Rolls with all the purdah curtains up, practically no air, the car had been full of mothballs for months and smelt awful.' They drove first to the Palace where the Nizam's troops shuffled past in 'ill-fitting uniforms and out of step. Old men and young men and a band incongrously playing "Onward Christian Soldiers" very badly.' She found it all 'rather pathetic'. They then drove extremely slowly in the stuffy car to the grandfather's tomb on which the boys solemnly placed flowers and she got home 'very late and very bad-tempered'.

Children's tea parties proved an equal trial. While the youngsters played, the ladies sat on rows of chairs facing each other and were served with platefuls of 'stuff exactly like chickenfeed and bananas and gaudy-coloured drinks' that she refused to touch. There was much rivalry between these wealthy ladies, one of whom told Margaret she employed no less than three English governesses and twenty ayahs to bring up and educate her seven children.

Altogether it was a rather inconsequential and haphazard sort of life, but Miss Ussher enjoyed it though she never had enough money and was grateful to one old

Maharajah who (after throwing coins to beggars from his car on the way to the palace) slipped her a half-sovereign when he left. A more highly-prized perk was the 'little blue-grey Hillman Minx' which the Begum bought her to drive to the Secundarabad Club. That made her feel very grand and independent, even though it looked rather insignificant beside the large Rolls, the Silver Rolls and the old Ford in the Begum's stable-garage.

The Begum, who 'was very keen on English customs' was a widow and Margaret suspected that the married Indian women of similar rank were rather jealous of her comparative independence. But the Begum didn't enjoy much freedom from the Nizam's influence, and it is quite surprising to learn that he allowed the Annual Conference of the Indian Women's Association to be held in the grounds of his own palace in 1939. Women delegates from all parts of the country attended and were put up in tents on the tennis courts.

The Conference President was the Nizam's old aunt who, Margaret wrote, 'had never attended a public meeting before in her life'. She arrived at the Conference hall 'with five or six slaves trailing behind her, each carrying bundles of water-pots, *pan*, spittoons etc. You never saw such a funny cavalcade processing up any platform! Finally they were installed, the slaves squatting about opening their bundles – some with their mortars and pestles making *pan*, another jumping up and down with the spittoon quite regardless of the fact that the Conference was in progress and that the various speakers were trying to make themselves heard by a big audience in the hall below. It was like a scene from the Middle Ages.'

Exactly thirty years had passed since Miss Florence Wyld walked into that neglected, unpromising, 'school' on Mount Charles with its few desks, its tattered *Royal Readers*. At that time the very concept of an Indian Women's Conference being held in the Nizam's grounds would have seemed an incredible miracle. In Miss

Ussher's rather undiscerning eyes it might have looked comic and medieval, but had Miss Wyld been there she would surely have been proud of the Nizam's old aunt!

2

The Old Red Carpet Days

> Some of the older generation of women
> 'became very very grand indeed, you know –
> ships in full sail – but except amongst the few
> women who took themselves very seriously, on
> the whole everyone knew that it was just a
> little bit of play-acting.'
>
> Nancy Vernede

The glittering rituals of the Raj seem to us like plays, or perhaps more a series of tableaux vivants, performed on that piece of red carpet rolled out for every occasion. The principal cast of actors, the majority of them male, moved with stately step from one performance to the next and in a manner that induced boredom rather than drama. The performances were static and repetitive, so that a description of one grand vice-regal function sounds almost identical to one of ten or even twenty years later. Never-theless, female visitors from Home or the remote upcountry stations were usually thrilled by so much splendour and extravagance – 'like something out of the Arabian Nights', or 'like an enchanted fairyland.' In retrospect, they can scarcely believe they actually saw such spectacles.

The great durbars early in the century were the very summit and apogee of such magnificence – an exuberant mingling of Eastern and Western ceremonial. For the Indians 'loved a show' as much as the British and each maharaja vied to outshine his neighbour. At the Delhi Durbar their vast reception tents were lined with purple, emerald and pale pink silks, luxuriously carpeted, wreathed with flowers and strings of coloured lights. It was a marvellous evening's entertainment to drive the three glittering miles along Coronation Road in carriages drawn by camels or elephants draped in jewelled regalia to 'see the Illuminations of the Native Princes'.

After the durbar of 1911 the building of New Delhi began, and Mrs Gladys Straus can remember playing among its foundations when a child. She and her parents lived for two years in huge tents equipped with permanent cemented fireplaces, and when they eventually moved to 'a proper bungalow along Queen Mary's Avenue', the fireplaces were left to crumble slowly away on the empty plain – a bizarre addition to the city's many ruins. Mrs Iris Portal, whose fascination with Indian history was first prompted by those ruins, used often to ride out to the still-wild countryside beyond where one could see, 'the occasional herd of black buck and peafowl everywhere'.

It was the early 1920s, and she was living in Old Delhi with her parents. On one occasion they made an expedition to New Delhi, 'then only about a foot high', accompanied by Sir Edwin Lutyens, the principal architect of the rising capital. He was, 'a funny old geezer who pranced around flirting with my mother', while her father, Sir Montagu Butler, 'sulked horribly'. Lutyens said he was particularly pleased with designs for the new staff bungalows which had central octagonal hallways with eight doors leading from them. Some doors led to the bedrooms and, he added with shrieks of laughter, would lead to much amusement during house parties, 'with guests not knowing which doors to go in or out of – while two led only into broom cupboards'.

The new capital was not officially inaugurated until 1931 and was an occasion for much 'red-carpeting'. Mrs Le Brocq, whose father was on the Council of State, remembers that 'We dined in the Viceroy's house off gold plates and there was this wonderful roof which went back and had a sort of blue velvet sky powdered with stars above. Oh it was tremendous! We stayed in the old Cecil Hotel, but we saw the whole opening procession coming down Kingsway

– and the carriages and the gold umbrellas – and it was something I shall never forget.'

During the 1930s, the guests of the Viceroy in Delhi enjoyed temporary bit-parts in an ongoing pageant that was also magnificently unforgettable. Mrs Janet Wright, who stayed in Government House at the time, remembers it just like that. After some preliminary polite chat, 'We found our partners and proceeded slowly and to music into the dining-room. My partner was Mr C.E. Rhodes, CIE; ICS . . . on my other side was Major-General M. Saunders, CB; DSO . . . What a show! Sixty-eight guests and we ate off silver plates! I didn't take my gloves off, just the hands because this was what Her Excellency Lady Linlithgow did.' After the usual toasts to the King-Emperor and the inevitable sumptuous desserts, came the signal for the ladies to retire and that, too, was like a 'stately minuette, curtseying at the door and going out in pairs'.

For the next scene, Her Excellency repaired to the State Drawing Room, explained Pamela Hinkson, who was a Viceregal guest a year later. She 'sits on a sofa and various ladies are led up to talk to her, each for a few minutes. Other ladies sit on chairs arranged in pairs or on sofas conversing in some way until the gentlemen join them. Then the same procedure follows. Ladies and gentlemen are led up one after another to talk to their Excellencies – a lady to the Viceroy, a gentleman to the Vicereine – and an ADC brings a gentleman up to each lady, introduces him and leaves him for the regulation time, when he is moved on and another takes his place.' Such procedures must have been specially designed to preclude the holding of any interesting conversation with anyone.

The Viceroy and his lady often held balls, one of which Janet Wright attended. 'Their Excellencies made their entrance about the fourth dance. The music stopped and the dancers divided into two sections with an open passage down the length of the room. Bugles sounded and their Excellencies were announced. She looked very lovely. He tired and grave. They proceeded with ADC's before and after them to the alcove at the top of the room. Alcoves on either side were labelled "House Party" and "Commander-in-Chief" on one side and "Ruling Princes" on the other.' After so much cosmopolitan splendour, it's rather pleasing to learn that, when Mrs Wright finally got to bed in the early hours, she could hear jackals howling – reminding the city's inhabitants of the newness of its walls, the antiquity of its earlier ruins.

On the mornings after the balls, Government House was cleansed, polished, redecorated for the forthcoming attractions. Miss Hinkson notes that 'something like 370 flower vases are filled afresh each day. Great jars of pink and white peach and almond blossom light the passages and spread their loveliness against the pale green walls of the pleasant room where tea is set at two round tables as in an English country house. A bank of orange-flower-scented narcissi floods the air with its sweetness. Flowers on the dining-table are changed for every meal. There are twenty *malis* whose special business it is to arrange the flowers for the house. They come across the garden in the early morning sunlight on the way from the cutting garden making a picture as they walk carrying their flowers; a great basket of mixed colour poised against their *pugrees* of bright orange.'

This was during the 'Delhi Season' when guests were so numerous that they overflowed the houses and were put up in fully-furnished, electrically-lit tents on the lawns. And it was often quite a problem to get them all properly dressed and assembled on the right stage at the right time – for *they*, after all, were mainly amateurs! So, Pamela Hinkson continues, there was 'frequently a soft tap at the door and a message of some kind from the ADC's room – a printed card with the name of each house-party guest on it, to be duly initialled as having been received and noted – giving, perhaps, the hour at which guests are requested to assemble before a State Dinner Party that night and the information that decorations – or gloves for ladies – will be worn. The special *chaprassis* in charge of these notices have a hard time running all the guests to earth and if they fail to find them in their rooms they lie in wait for them in the garden, catching them as they come from or to the tennis-courts, appearing suddenly from behind an orange tree to salaam and hold out the card and pencil . . .'

Pure Alice in Wonderland that – a world with its own rituals of etiquette, its own brand of logic. Girls whose fathers held high-ranking posts in India had to learn the rules when their formal education ended. They were taught how to behave at dinner parties ('talk first to the man on your right; then to the man on your left; start a conversation but never close it; never shut up either man'), always to wear long white gloves at, for instance, Simla's Gaiety Theatre; always to carry frilly parasols to race-meetings; to invite to parties only young men who had officially 'called' . . . and so on. It all sounds preposterous to us now and much further away in time than it actually was.

To bring that distant red-carpet world within our present-day compass we might look at a few of the backstage arrangements instead of the upfront glitter. It's the sort of detail we can best glean from women's memoirs, for the leading men were too busy and too dignified to bother about such matters. Miss Yvonne Fitzroy, a private secretary to Lady Alice Reading when she was Vicereine between 1921 and 1925, had 'a weakness for a show', but also gives glimpses of how that show actually got on the road, and the personal costs of keeping it there.

She and Lady Reading used to make a tour of inspection prior to the holding of a Viceregal ball to see all was proceeding smoothly – such as the polishing of the vast ballroom floor. 'Up and down the room six boys pulled a flat wooden sledge, at the top of which reposed a heavy granite slab and on the top of the slab a very old man, turbanned and cross-legged, holding a tin of chalk which he

33

sprinkled in front of him as he went. Every time he got to the end of the room the boys whisked the sledge round and upset both his balance and his temper.' But he soon rearranged himself and they were off again.

The ball on that occasion was to be at the Viceregal Lodge in Simla and on the night (21 May 1921) the band's platform was banked with flowers – magenta bougainvillea, scarlet geraniums, purple canterbury bells. The ballroom verandah was screened with red hangings and 'carpets gallantly doing their best to appear of the same colour, led the way to the supper room – a transformed Council Chamber'. It so happened that the Indian leader, Mahatma Gandhi, was in Simla just then with an appointment to see Lord Reading and 'Tom-toms and cries of greeting had floated up' towards the Lodge heralding his arrival while Lady Reading prolonged her inspection tour in order to catch a glimpse of him. And, at the appointed hour, the already legendary leader duly appeared. He was skinny, bent, clad in simple white cotton – a spectral, incongruous figure – who yet walked with dignity past the banked flowers, the decorated ballroom and on into the Viceroy's sanctum. 'Sometimes it seems strange how undisturbedly the machinery of life goes on side by side with issues which one feels – though ignorantly – to be so far-reaching', comments Miss Fitzroy later. But that night the show went on as usual, the garden was a sparkle of Chinese lanterns, His and Her Excellencies sat at opposite ends of the great ballroom 'while all Simla pranced before them'.

A great deal of prancing went on in Simla; it seemed 'like a set for a musical comedy', remarked Mrs Olive Crofton who first visited it in the late 1920s. 'The ladies dressed up to the nines in rickshaws along the Mall, civilians in tail coats and white topees, red-tabbed staff officers, black-trousered hill-men and women with baskets of flowers and bundles of grass on their backs' – and all, surely, about to burst into a chorus proclaiming the joys of hill-station life!

When Yvonne Fitzroy accompanied 'Her Ex' to an important Simla function they rode in 'an open britzka like Queen Victoria used to drive in, with postillions in scarlet, gold and white breeches, the Head Coachman in scarlet and gold before us, the Bodyguard mounted, the ADCs each side of us – altogether a very fine show.'

Probably the showiest show of the regular Simla season was the Black Hearts Ball, given by the community's most confirmed and respected bachelors, who geared themselves up for the occasion in scarlet capes with large black hearts on the left side and black-heart lockets suspended from scarlet ribbons round their necks. The Readings, who introduced more informality into society generally, got up 'A Cotillon for the Black Hearts' in return.

'The favours [sprays of feathers and artificial flowers] arrived from Paris in the last mail and are delicious,' Miss Fitzroy reported. She and Lady Reading spent the morning arranging them in the ballroom, 'with the invaluable and experienced help of Captain Sassoon'. Lady Reading made some of the ribbon whips and helped with the sewing of bells on reins. The Black Hearts seemed a trifle nervous on first arrival, but soon everyone got into the swing of things and 'It was colossal! Reverend gentlemen renowned hitherto for their eloquence in the Legislative Assembly . . . raced the length of the ballroom on cushions – danced in solitary defeat blowing gold bugles – wore paper rosette headdresses the wrong way up – tore round room in teams of four to the strains of John Peel and everyone was hallooing – bleating like sheep or roaring like lions – and from beginning to end laughing without ceasing.' For the finale, a sleigh piled with favours and flowers was drawn in by a team of eight, 'downfalls of "snowflakes" and confetti were thrown about and then everyone played "Follow my Leader" through the house in a condition of breathless but delighted collapse.' After the guests left about four in the morning, Miss Fitzroy repaired to the ADC's room for black beer and sandwiches.

Miss Yvonne Fitzroy was quite elevated in the social hierarchy of course; she attended many social functions and travelled with the Readings. Not for her the concerns of the English domestic staff who supervised the army of Indian servants that actually maintained the ruling establishments at their various levels of splendour.

The residences of the three British governors were second only to the Viceroy's in degrees of splendour – as is evident from a graphic backstage account given by one Mrs Tyler. She became housekeeper and lady's maid to the Lumleys in Bombay soon after the governess, Miss Flaas, had left to get married – in the manner of her kind.

Mrs Tyler had been trained in dressmaking, hairdressing and art needlework and had a proven record of competence in household management before she joined the establishment in Bombay. The 'native staff' was made up of Hindus, Moslems and Goanese who 'all worked in harmony', according to her; they included two full-time upholsterers, two full-time tailors and a Goanese head-linen-man one of whose jobs was to repair (every day!) the Union Jack which went up the flagstaff at sunrise and came down at sunset.

The housekeeper's day began soon after the flag went up, 'on the dot of seven'. First she checked all the public rooms in the various bungalows to see that the *hammels* were up and about their appointed tasks. These were the housemen who cleaned, dusted and polished and one could tell who did what by the slightly differing cuts of their uniforms. At eight she called Sir Roger and Lady Lumley and then had her own breakfast. The head tailor arrived at nine and settled down on his red-tiled verandah. Getting his own blanket from his own cupboard, he then 'spread a beautiful clean sheet over it . . . The machine always stood in the corner ready for use and he'd proceed with whatever job he had to do and I must say he never had a pattern. All the patterns were made by him under my instruction. I did all the fitting and really he was wonderful. I can't tell you all the things we made for the four young ladies and Her Excellency. All the children's underwear, most of the day dresses, fancy dresses, evening dresses, even suits he could make . . .'

Clothes were a daily preoccupation, for she had also to supervise the bearers who ironed them and she always 'did gloves and stockings for Her Excellency . . . for if they were roughly handled they wouldn't last'. She also kept a record of Her Ladyship's wardrobe so she didn't wear the same rig-out to the same place.

Later in the morning she helped Her Ladyship dress and then went to supervise the *dhobies* collecting the house-linen for washing. On an ordinary day this amounted to one and a half dozen bathtowels, three dozen pillowcases, ditto napkins, ten tablecloths . . . and so on. Frequently, people would be moving in or out of the various bungalows, and that meant sending for the PWD men to check the furniture, the plumbing and the paintwork, and calling in upholsterers to repair covers and cushions.

Mrs Tyler had an hour off in the afternoons and then it was back to check the public rooms again and lay out all the clothes for 'the evening dressings'. Each of the Governor's households had its own band which usually played through-out the dinner hour. Mrs Tyler's husband was the bandmaster and leader of those 'bandy boys' who went to wine and dine at Nanny's on their nights off. Mr Tyler wore a 'splendid uniform with epaulettes and a sun helmet with spike wings and three gilt stripes on each arm' (though he said that the epaulettes were a 'confounded nuisance' when he was playing pizzicato passages). He was usually up till all hours, for people dined late, but one imagines that his wife often crept early to bed, for she had another busy day ahead.

An experienced housekeeper, Mrs Tyler was quite used to the luxurious trappings of the wealthy and powerful British, but she was utterly bowled over when she accompanied the Lumleys to visit the domains of the Maharaja of Baroda. 'I could hardly believe my eyes,' she said. 'What with the processions of the royal elephants, the flocks of snow-white peacocks, the antics of the tame tumbling pigeons, a garden laid out like a Willow Pattern tea-set and guns embossed in gold and silver.' It was a sentiment shared by many of her compatriots for whom the luxurious world of Indian royalty was astounding, exotic and spectacular beyond reasonable belief.

Foreign males were forbidden entry into the women's quarters of this regal world – *zenanas*, as the British usually called them – and so it was left to their womenfolk to describe their cloistered but equally exotic and wondrous rituals. Miss Florence Wyld, for instance, felt herself especially privileged because she was the only foreigner to receive an annual invitation from 'Lady K.', the wife of a high-ranking Hyderabad official, to celebrate her son's birthday. On arrival Miss Wyld was ushered into a large courtyard with a deep recess along one side. Here, the visiting begums were reclining on cushions in expectation of Lady K. whose 'arrival was heralded by the faint sound of pipes from a corner of the courtyard beyond'. Then a column of eight girls appeared, playing softly on a little instrument like a flute and called apparently The Amazon Band. Behind them . . . came Lady K., short but dignified, wearing a most beautiful sari.' She was escorted by an attendant 'who carried a baby tiger cradled comfortably in her arms'.

Once regally settled among special cushions on the other side of the reception hall, Lady K. would summon the ladies to come and converse with her in turns and for short intervals; but what the tiger did Miss Wyld does not, unfortunately, tell us. Later in the evening, the arrival of the birthday son was announced and the begums scurried away behind screens, but Miss Wyld firmly stayed put, her presence being tactfully ignored. Male attendants appeared to scatter gold-embroidered cushions and reverently unroll lengths of golden carpet on which trod the Nawab and his son, arrayed in positive 'breastplates of diamonds'.

Dancing girls performed for their entertainment and then, after the men had left, the begums popped out from behind the screens and fell to eating, drinking and chatting. To Miss Wyld's surprise most of them made no move to leave but simply stayed, growing drowsier, quieter and eventually falling asleep on their cushions. One year Florence stayed too and, in the middle of the night, went up alone to the flat roof above the courtyard where she sat for a long while contemplating the stars above, the slumbering women below.

Mrs M. Ravenscroft gives a hilarious account of a coming of age festival for a local raja during which the red carpet literally slipped. The District Commissioner was there with his aides, the Head of Police and 'all the heaven-born lady wives who had to go to be received by the Ranee, and I had to tail along with them. There were about sixteen ladies, all rather elderly, very proper and conscious that they were, you know, responsible people and representing the British Raj, and most of them had been very well trained by their husbands.' She was young at the time, recently married, and 'I felt the whole thing was utterly beyond me, I couldn't cope at all'.

Before the presentation, the ladies had rather too small garlands of marigolds rammed down by servants over their very large broad-brimmed hats and after it they were released onto 'a sort of parade ground round the ladies' palace on two levels. We were on the upper one and had to go down a flight of marble steps to the lower and quite suddenly, just as we were approaching the steps, somebody remembered their manners and fetched a roll of red carpet and hastily laid it down, but not pushing it in each step with anything safe . . . And the senior lady advanced to the top and managed the first two or three steps then her heel caught and there were cascades of ladies coming down those steps. I was the last, enjoying it to the bitter end as

their anguished husbands below darted forward to receive
their tottering forms. I've never seen anything so funny in
all my life!'

That particular occasion was memorable for its mirth;
similar ones were usually solemn and tedious – especially
when only women were present. Few of either race could
speak the other's language, so there were embarrassing
silences of mutual incomprehension, uncertainties about
what to do and when to leave. Mrs Ravenscroft makes no
bones about how uneasy she felt visiting the Ranee of Alwa
who 'probably thought I was just as weird as I thought she
was'. She was first escorted upstairs to 'a hideous room,
very long and narrow and lined with hideous pictures, the
sort you look full face at and it's one face and you go to the
other side and it's somebody else's face – awful trick
pictures. There was a very long table and two rows of
chairs, of Victorian mahogany and very plush, and there
you were dumped and you sat and attendant ladies came
and squirted you liberally with attar of roses – drenched
you in it. When I got home I always took off all my clothes
and sent them straight to the laundry; some things I could
never wear again, I couldn't get the smell out.'

Eventually the Ranee came in '. . . and sat stolidly down
and you'd say the few correct words you knew, and she'd
say hers and you'd sit there and she'd clear her throat very
loudly and noisily, sort of sniff and snort quite a lot, so
you'd just bow gently. And occasionally a question would
be asked which you might understand or not but you did
your best and after a while she gave a signal and you went
home thankfully. Not very exciting. Quite often she tried to
give you a present which you just bowed over and
gracefully said, "No, I couldn't." So she had it wrapped up
and her servant trotted behind you all the way home and
when you got there you handed the present to your
husband who said a few correct things and returned it to
the servant who trotted back to the palace with it. This was
just routine.'

*

One was also expected to visit the local rajas when on tour. And it could be somewhat fatiguing to find, on arrival at your tent after a long day's journey, that you had to pretty yourself up in full evening dress with the aid of a small cracked mirror and a dressing-case perched on a trunk, and sally forth to a banquet at the nearby palace. Invariably men and women were separated and in the latter's quarters conversation seldom sparkled, even when one could manage the language. Dorothy Middleton, whose father was Governor of the Central Provinces, remembers accompanying her mother to visit the five wives of the Raja in the remote state of Sarguja. 'Their quarters were decorated with gimcrack ornaments, notably a little jewelled clock which had stopped and which was, I thought, symbolic of their deadly lives. Mother and I talked of the weather and admired their clothes. Then the Raja came to fetch us away – to drive the hundred yards or so back to our camp in his Rolls Royce, driven by a handsome bearded Sikh. The car stuck fast in the first few yards, but my mother was quite equal to the situation and chatted serenely to our host until out of the bushes appeared a squad of nearly naked Gonds (the local tribesmen) who pushed us, still making conversation, silently back to our tents!'

Incidentally, the coming of the motorcar did something to broaden the horizons of those purdah wives whose husbands could afford to buy them. While a pupil of Auckland House School Simla during the 1930s, Pat Frost went to stay with her friend, a princess of the royal family of Patiala. The degree of restriction imposed on its younger members depended 'on the whim of the elderly Ranee – which I accepted without much question, as schoolgirls do'. For a special treat and after much preparation, a shopping expedition to Delhi was occasionally allowed. The ladies rode 'in a stately cavalcade of closed motor cars, driven by uniformed chauffeurs who were all eunuchs'. Having been warned of their coming, 'a block of shops in

Connaught Circus was cleared of all its ordinary customers and a corridor of screens was put up from shops to car and the princesses were escorted inside'. When they'd taken their pick of the wares on display – usually without any regard to cost – the process was repeated in the next block.

Purdah ladies had to be served by female staff only. Marjorie Williamson, an assistant manageress in the Army and Navy Stores, Calcutta, remembers the store being specially opened for them on Sunday mornings – which was a real drag for her and her colleagues in the ladies' departments at the end of a long week. 'They bought up anything and everything, just for the sake of buying, just for the fun of being in a store.' One didn't have to sell; the ladies 'simply picked up objects of every kind, put them on one side and servants carried them away to their motor cars.' That part was easy; apparently it was sometimes more difficult to get the maharajahs to pay their bills!

Those among the British community who had the most regular and close contact with the households of Indian royalty were the Residents, whose job it was to keep an eye on conditions within each Native State. Their wives undoubtedly endured many ceremonial longueurs, but it was perfectly splendid to be the seventeen-year-old daughter of a Resident seeing the Indian side of the red carpet for the first time. Betsy Macdonald, whose mother sent her little parcels smelling of India, was the daughter of the Resident of Neemuch. After that dreary boarding-school life, her first year back with her parents was 'like a glamorous fairytale', and the pinnacle of the glamour was the visits they made to several Native States.

The entertainment was 'fabulous. We watched jugglers, musicians, dancers and the private individual armies of the Princes in all manner of unique uniforms. The halls in which banquets were held were stupendous pillared rooms, some with colourful scenes depicting the ancient days and former rulers, others with magnificent embroidered hangings, fine lattice screens, cut-glass chandeliers and mirrors making a dazzling effect. For the diners, long tables were laid with spotless white cloths laden with gold and silver plate, immense bowls of fruit, cleverly festooned with exotic flowers.'

At these banquets the diners would be seated before the Maharajah appeared 'surrounded by his courtiers. They were all resplendently dressed, their long coats looking like cloths of gold. Each one would wear different headgear according to his caste and these creations would have made any milliner proud, adorned as they were with fabulous jewels and feathers. Immediately dozens of servants would appear bearing elaborate dishes.' Afterwards guests were entertained with the performances of dancing girls, but what Betsy most enjoyed 'was sitting on rooftops or in the gardens in the cool, clear moonlight, listening to the Indian music, singers or musicians holding the instruments they played across their knees'.

Another girl of similar age who thoroughly enjoyed her visits to a Native State was Monica Clough, whose father had now become General Manager of thirty tea estates in Trevancore. Consequently, the Cloughs were often invited to functions held by the Royal House in Trivandrum. A foretaste of splendours to come was suggested by the invitation cards 'beautifully engraved with an heraldic emblazon of two elephants holding up a conch shell'. Because Trevancore was independent, the senior planters felt themselves representatives of Empire and the two races met 'with very little stuffiness or criticism of each other'.

The drawbacks of these visits were having to wear elbow-length white kid gloves in such heat and to munch one's way through long, heavy meals while His Highness and his entourage sat 'with two limes each on their gilt plates which they sniffed occasionally' in lieu of eating. But then came the pleasure – three-hour concerts of South Indian music. 'The players sat on a central dais and the leader somehow managed to conduct with his eyebrows' while Monica sat on a special gilt chair, clutching the bouquet of jasmine always presented to her. Her parents found the performances fairly excruciating, but she, 'having no fully-formed western preconceptions of musicality' was enthralled. Those concerts and royally elaborate performances of Kathkali dances 'opened a door for me into a different India.'

Trevancore was an eighteen-gun state, meaning that its ruler merited a gun-salute of that number on ceremonial occasions; this was superior, but not quite in the class of Kashmir – a twenty-one-gun state. In the late 1930s, Desirée Battye went out to Kashmir as Personal Assistant to its Resident – and was immediately and enormously impressed by it all. She was met at Rawalpindi by a chauffeur wearing a red-and-gold braided turban who saluted her and ushered her into the Resident's car. 'With the two servants sitting in front of the black Vauxhall saloon, the flag of the same red and gold flying bravely before, I sat grandly back, thrilled with my elevated position, wishing some of the girls at St James's Secretarial College in London could see me now!' When the chauffeur blew his horn to clear a path through the villages, chickens and goats scattered and children waved as they recognized the flag. Eventually they drove under an imposing arched gateway – and there was the Residency, reputedly one of the most beautiful in the whole Empire.

It looked 'just like a large English country house set in an English garden with spacious, soft green lawns, shady trees and sweeping, colourful herbaceous borders'. The trees were chenar, walnut, apricot and the red Kashmiri apple; among their branches and over the weedless lawns fluttered rosy starlings, golden orioles and green parrots with long yellow tails. The house was two-storeyed, with flowery creepers cascading over an arcaded porch, a facade of crisscross beams, a gabled roof and long covered balconies. Its main rooms were 'the size of four ordinary ones', and the most beautiful was the drawing room to the left of the entrance. Here were 'many French windows framed in deep pink brocade curtains leading on one side to a balcony. The room had a turquoise ceiling that picked out the colour from an unusual circular carpet made by Haddows of Srinagar which lay in the room's centre. Everywhere there were vases, several attached to the pale pink walls between the windows, trailing flowers and greenery, others on tables beside silver-framed photographs of bejewelled Maharajahs.'

In charge of this grand establishment – from Desirée herself to the dogs' own sweeper – were Sir Denholm Fraser and his wife Sheila, the 'Lady Sahib', who welcomed her warmly. Her initial description of them is vividly detailed, even though they emerge as somehow too perfect, too typical – like characters in some polite drawing room comedy of the period. Sir Denholm ('Dem') was 'slim and boyish in grey flannel trousers, yellow and maroon Central India Horse tie and ancient light-tweed jacket, looking incredibly young for his fifty years in spite of his peppered military moustache and greying hair. His wife Sheila had put on a considerable amount of weight since bearing three sons in rapid succession, but her face was like a girl's, skin like a peach, features lovely in their classical beauty of full lips and glinting brown hair . . . twisted into a chignon. She liked to dress in bright, youthful colours, her still-slender legs clad in sheer silk stockings, feet encased in high-heeled, open-work shoes.'

From the start Desirée loved every minute of every day. She was wakened early by her ayah, 'with a fresh-picked flower in her hair, bringing a tray of *chota hazri* (little breakfast) and throwing open wide the shutters of the French windows to let the sun stream into my room. I would step out on to my balcony, sniffing the scented air from the white jasmine creeping over the lintel and listening to the sounds of the nearby bazaar. Wooden steps led down through the shrubbery in the back garden to a small gate leading out through the willow trees to the

crowded Bund along the Jhelum river. In one corner of the
balcony, the *chowkidar*'s blankets were neatly folded into a
pile ready for his next night's vigil, which, in spite of his
snores, did seem to ensure we were not burgled.'

Back in the bedroom, the ayah had prepared everything
for her comfort, even to 'squeezing out a quarter-inch of
toothpaste' for her use, sprinkling her bath water with
sandalwood oil and was waiting to scrub her back and give
her a massage. After breakfast came the ritual of 'Bringing
in the Book' – that is, the Visitors' Book which was handed
to the Lady Sahib every morning 'and studied to see if
anyone of interest had signed. Everyone who signed would
be asked to something, their names typed out under
headings: Dinner, Luncheon, Buffet Lunch, Tea and
Tennis, Cocktails, all according to rank, the least being
cocktails'. Then the invitations were written out and given
to a *chaprassi* to deliver by hand. One wonders if those
invited to mere cocktails knew they were among 'the least'?

Desirée's duties were not onerous, consisting, on the
secretarial side, mainly of taking down and typing 'secret'
letters which the Resident didn't want to go through the
normal channel of the Indian secretariat. These, he
explained to her, were to do with defence, plans for coping
with emergencies or private letters to the Maharajah. Her
other daily task was pure enjoyment: the arranging of fresh
flowers in all the main rooms. Lady Fraser, an expert
herself, taught her how best to display 'the lovely sprays
and blossoms culled from the garden into different shapes
and colour schemes' for the low-spreading arrangements
on the long dining table of polished walnut, handmade by
Kashmiri craftsmen.

In the evenings, Desirée acted as 'second hostess . . . to
help make the parties go', though it wasn't always easy to
infuse shy Indian ladies with the right party spirit and they
tended to 'dry up completely when addressed by the
Resident'. After the lengthy dinners, ending, often, with
her favourite savoury of angels-on-horseback, 'flaked

almonds embedded in a prune enveloped in crisp bacon on a golden crunch of fried bread', the gentlemen separated from the ladies and went out 'on the lawns to water the borders. Apparently this after-the-Mess-dinner relic still carried on, though they passed a modern Gents on the way to the garden. It struck me as an extraordinarily crude ending to a most civilized meal!' After coffee, often served outdoors, the guests departed; the moon shone on the high fields of wild white roses in the distant hills, the *chowkidar* unfolded his blankets on the balcony and slept. And next day the stately Residential rhythms began again: fresh flowers were gathered, the Visitors' Book was scrutinized and new guests arrived – flustered, bored, pompous – to play their little walk-on parts.

Occasionally, wearying of their leading roles, the Resident and his staff took a few hours off and floated down-river in their private gondola. Its hull was painted green and gold, 'with curtains tied back at four corners, which could be pulled across for privacy. Overhead were awnings canopied in scarlet and yellow. We sat back on the brightly cushioned seats feeling like something out of Omar Khayyam and watched the Residential flag open out as the four boatmen in scarlet liveries stood behind in the stern, propelling the boat out to mid-stream with long-handled paddles . . .'

3

The Junglies

'I used to be absolutely petrified, coming
down for our fortnight's Christmas leave into
society. I was simply a woman of the bush, or
you might call it the jungle. And one put on
evening dress every night, but one felt like a
sort of Cinderella . . . I just felt I couldn't fit in.
I simply loathed it.'

Mrs Olivia Hamilton

Hundreds of British women who lived in India during the
period came no nearer to the royal red carpets than the
average English housewife to a ball at Buckingham Palace.
Some of them were the wives of police, forestry or political
officers, of mining engineers, surveyors, geologists who
lived in extremely isolated regions. They travelled through
jungles and across mountains, lived in frontier outposts, in
tribal territories and deserts where transport was a matter
of bullock carts, horses, camels, elephants, river boats; for
months on end they lived in tents, in ramshackle forestry
bungalows or guarded fortresses. They had a very limited
social life and only occasional access to amenities such as
shops, libraries, hairdressers, doctors or dentists – for a
nearby dentist is indeed an amenity if, as Mrs Hamilton
once did, you have to ride a hundred and sixty miles to get a
tooth pulled.

Like Mrs Hamilton, many of these women felt quite
estranged from and intimidated by the ordinary social
rituals of their compatriots – who often dubbed them (and
their husbands) as 'junglies'. It was spoken half in jest, for
the only thoroughgoing junglies were the few British men
who 'went completely native'. These hinterland junglies

48

didn't go to such extremes, but they were certainly rather odd; they knew more about India than perhaps was good for them and, even more oddly, they seemed rather to enjoy their isolation.

Indeed there were many compensations in the jungly lifestyle if, like Mrs Hamilton, you were a healthy, self-sufficient type of person with a love of the great outdoors. Her husband Arthur, not 'a clubby sort of man' either, was an Assistant Divisional Forestry Officer with headquarters in Lahore. When she first joined him there, just three months after their marriage, she was given a wedding present of a silver tray engraved with the names of all the forestry officers in the Punjab.

In early spring, as soon as the mountain roads were passable, the Hamiltons set off together from Simla to the Kulu District in the Himalayas. They wore their up-country clothes which, for her, meant breeches, lace-up canvas gaiters and deerskin boots, a tweed jacket and a topee to cover her short-cropped hair. Mules carried their camping equipment and nearly a year's supply of essentials such as medicines, stationery and enamelled-iron crockery which was unbreakable. There was good reason for this: the mules' large loads stuck out on either side of their bodies and were sometimes wider than the narrow mountain roads. At dangerous corners, 'the mule-men would get hold of the mule's tail and pull it towards the cliff-side as the animal went slowly round, so that, if its foot slipped over the edge, he could haul it back'.

The cook, who baked good bread, carried yeast in a tied-down bottle round his own neck because it was so precious. For any special supplies had to be ordered from Lahore, 'took two weeks to come and cost the earth'. So they lived 'off the country' which was pleasant enough once you got the knack of it – and the knack was bred in Olivia Hamilton's bones, for she came from a family with generations of Indian connections and her mother had been born in a tent on the North-West frontier.

While Mr Hamilton was busy surveying vast tracts of forest they lived for weeks on end in camps set up in a small clearing or on a steep slope. One of Olivia's first duties at each new site was to 'turn over every stone all round each tent to see how many scorpions I could kill from underneath before they got into our slippers or our beds'. The cook meanwhile would be making his fireplace, building his fire and sending a bearer to buy charcoal from the nearest settlement. That cook had an inborn instinct for the life too and had learned recipes 'handed down to his family from our grandparents through generations of cooks'. He never wrote out a recipe; they were all in his memory and he could produce a good meal from very little at any time of day or night.

After the evening meal (often of green pigeon or pheasant they'd shot for the pot), Mr Hamilton usually settled in his office tent to 'write and write till all hours' by the light of a hurricane lamp, while his wife occupied herself with tying fish-flies. 'I was rather good at it. I used to collect feathers – from game birds, cocks and so on – quite obsessively and make up the flies to order. I sent them as far away as Kashmir sometimes and I once bought myself an evening dress on the proceeds.'

Late at night, 'we always sat up round the camp-fire and one of the delights would be to see the flying squirrels who loved the smell of the smoke, coming down from a tree and floating through the smoke down to the base of another tree, and then they'd run up that tree and fly back and down again. A beautiful sight.' When camping higher up near the Tibetan plateau they used to shoot and skin birds for their collector friends in Simla. 'We used a little $8' \times 8'$ Everest tent then and it was frequent for us to be sleeping one on each side and in between us there would be a pair of seagulls or black-necked crane or hooded crow that I was in the process of skinning.'

Early in the morning at those high altitudes they might waken to the weird, beautiful call of the rare mariale pheasant that slept on the cliff edges. Sometimes they were fortunate enough to glimpse one: '. . . gliding down into the sunlight, the sheen of them with their crests is quite lovely'. All day they travelled through the mountainous forests hearing only the cries of the wild birds and, occasionally, 'a sawing noise that gets extremely loud and then dies away' – which was a panther on the roam and calling for a mate. The Hamiltons shot panthers sometimes and black bears too and certainly saw no harm in this, 'especially if the animals were harrying villagers or their possessions.' The hill women vowed that bears would not attack members of their sex, 'Just lift up your skirts and you'll be all right,' they told Olivia. But she found this hard to believe since the women sometimes turned up at her camp 'with torn arms or legs from bear attacks!'

Another characteristic sound of the region was the scuffling and baaing of great herds of sheep and goats leaving the plains to go to higher altitudes for the grazing. They moved in clouds of dust, guarded by dogs to protect them from predators and 'had little packs of tea and salt tied on them to take to the Tibetan borders.' As the Hamiltons descended past them on the way to the valleys they heard the grand rush of torrential rivers which they had to cross on rope bridges. These were no more than 'two cables of rope with hanging loops and when you put your foot on one and stepped forward, it went back and you had to find the other and you saw this enormous roaring river deep below. And as you got into the centre, your handle, or the rope cables got lower and lower and you swung up and down as well as from side to side. Really it was quite a hair-raising experience.'

But such hazards and discomforts did not deter Olivia from a life that had so much beauty and interest in it. 'We lived simply and had a very happy time in the hills', she affirms. She loved the natural grandeur of the region and the people who lived there, especially the peasant women with whom she had most contact. 'I have never seen such courage', she wrote of them. 'I have never seen such acceptance of terrible poverty, knowing nothing can ever help them really.' Yet, though mired in utter deprivation, 'they would always ask you to share their bed, share their home, to share their last bit of food or milk'.

How different it was in Simla, to which, after months of Himalayan solitude, they reluctantly returned. Her husband had by then grown a long shaggy beard which had to be hacked off as they approached 'civilization'. And, 'he looked priceless. Dark as a Tibetan above with his white chin below.' In fact, 'when we arrived in Simla with all those beautiful ladies beautifully dressed up, we felt really pretty awful. Just like a couple of hoboes!'

Mrs Hamilton was fortunate because she was able to enjoy the invigorating liberty of the forests without restraint or anxiety. Other wives found themselves in equally remote areas bordering the North-West Frontier that were frequently beset with territorial and border disputes. Even the Readings who visited the region in 1922 had to travel in an armoured car 'with an orderly on the box with a gun cocked'. They were informed that the neighbouring tribes were a rough lot, 'who shoot like we use a handkerchief.'

In these circumstances British wives could not be so carefree and mobile as the junglies of the Himalayas. Mrs M. Dench, wife of 'Will', a sub-divisional officer of the North-West Frontier Police, went out to Malakand just after the First World War and on her first journey there by hired car had to lie on the floor in the back because 'there was supposed to be snipers in the thorn-scrub'. The fort in which she spent the early months of her married life was 'barricaded from dawn to dusk. A high wall surrounded it and from each picket in its circumference alert eyes viewed the valley below, the ridge and the cart-road and plains to Yusufzai'. The whole atmosphere was relentlessly military. 'I awoke to the sound of bugle calls which continued at intervals during the day until the drummer beat the retreat and the bugles sounded again as the Union Jack on the parade ground came fluttering down. Then a solitary bugle sounded the Last Post which echoed and died away among the hills.'

The situation in the region was still tense when, in the early 1930s, Viola Bayley went to join her husband Vernon whom she'd married only a month after their first meeting. He too was in the Frontier Constabulary which had the job of keeping order between British India and the Tribal Territories, and, in the view of his young wife, the outposts he went to inspect were 'so like the mud fortresses of a Beau Geste film that, at first sight, they looked like cardboard'.

So the setting was romantic and she was fascinated by 'the larger than life scenery – the huge crags and scrub-covered hills and ravines that were our back-cloth'. She also found them somewhat 'intimidating because of their size and sense of desolation and because it was hard to forget that Tribal Territory – with its reputation for raids and skirmishes – was uncomfortably close to our back doorstep'. As she points out, for a girl like herself who had no previous connection with India and had been 'brought up in the security of a small Sussex town, it was a fairly traumatic experience to start married life in Hangu, a tiny link on the road that led from Peshawar to Kohat and Bannu and finally to the Khyber Pass'.

Two armed constables accompanied her and her new husband when they first walked out together, which was 'not conducive to the pleasure of a honeymoon stroll'. Many of the local tribesmen were Pathans who invariably carried rifles, and prisoners from the local jail (which was always full) were brought in under armed guard to make irrigation channels in their bungalow garden. Irrigation brought flowers in the spring, a season which 'was a revelation. Our violet bed stretched the length of our garden and scented the whole air. All along the valley there were orchards pink with peach blossom and carpeted with small iris. There were pink and white wild tulip and blue ixiolerion. There were oleanders flowering in the dry water-beds . . . We went on expeditions up the Khyber Pass as grim and impressive as I'd pictured it, but our picnic was by a stream where paradise flycatchers drifted in and out of birch trees with their exquisite floating motion. Hoopoes pecked at grubs on our lawn and bulbuls sang.'

During this propitious season Mrs Bayley often accompanied her husband on inspection visits to the constabulary posts tucked away in the foothills. And, 'When our car was sighted there was usually a race to wake the *subadah* in charge and there would be a great buttoning of uniforms and a clatter of constables falling in to time with our arrival. My chief memory of our one-night stays is this clatter of men falling in, falling out, hoicking of sentries on duty, the reek of curry, tough old roosters that appeared without fail for dinner to be reincarnated at our next meal; wonderful starlight nights, horrible hairy spiders and a general sense of complete unreality.'

In this remote, unreal-seeming mountain region British women had early learned the art of living off the country – even though they lived in commodious bungalows rather than cramped tents. Di Turner, whose father was also attached to the police, returned to the Frontier to live with her parents during the first world war. It was a rather large family, money was scarce and she and her mother made ingenious use of local products. They bought cartfuls of apricots and figs from the local farmers, made jams and chutneys, kept the seeds for cakes, laid some fruits to dry on the roof; they made marmalade from carrots, ginger and nuts, sliced and strung along the balconies green tomatoes and eggplants to dry for winter use. For family birthdays, they made 'strawberry jam from white figs tinted with strawberry essence' and for Christmas, they served crystallized peaches and blanched almonds. They collected sheep's wool from the hillsides, washed it thoroughly and used it as a padding for the sofas that they covered with cretonne.

By the 1930s, supplies of food were more easily obtainable, but housekeeping still presented problems especially when cook and memsahib shared no common language. Viola Bayley's first cook solved the difficulty 'of ordering meat by cutting the proposed joint on his own person, from brains to rumpsteak, involving fearsome contortions and wild guesswork on my part when it came to the miming of such things as oxtail or liver and kidneys'. The Bayleys grew fond of this ingenious cook, a 'disarmingly gentle soul' who was devoted to their Alsatian puppy, Susue. When the pup was ill, 'we had next to nothing to eat as cook remained seated in Susue's basket rocking her in his arms. It was impossible to get angry with him when he turned his mild grey eyes on one.' When her husband accused him of taking half the rice stock to feed his relatives, 'he remarked that he'd been under the impression we were all one big happy family. We found ourselves almost apologetic . . . Alas, he had one great failing. His cooking was atrocious!'

In the years between the sojourns of the Turners and the Bayleys, Mrs Dolly Rowe also did a stint of housekeeping on the Frontier. Her husband was a mining engineer busy with the construction of roads and water supplies and on first arrival she'd been rather frightened 'by all those tribal men, dressed up in yellow pushteens . . . tearing about on ponies, scattering everybody in their path. But nobody seemed to mind because there's no law there.' She soon got used to the tribesmen but not the local chappattis and was determined to make some proper bread. So she ordered hops from the brewery in Peshawar and 'added potatoes and a few sultanas and the occasional banana and poured boiling water on top' and 'put the mixture in two long bottles in front of the fire every night'; with this strange yeast she was able to bake bread which, though she said it herself, was pretty good.

The Rowes were also 'out-station people' by choice and enjoyed the pioneering outdoor life. Dolly accompanied her husband when he went to inspect the pipelines to make sure the local farmers hadn't tampered with the water flows. After the day's work they fished for silver trout in the Dugga River using 'a saucepan with no handle and a piece of cloth over the top with a hole in the middle and brown flour in the bottom, and the trout go in after it'. The trout didn't get out; the Rowes grilled them for supper over a campfire.

Some of their happiest excursions were on a motorbike, she riding in the side-car, 'which was very comfortable, with a place at the back for the luggage. I had a petrol can in front of me and the petrol sometimes scorched my legs'. In this fashion they once travelled from Peshawar to Lahore: 'It's cotton country there, you see. And the cotton is on the side of roads. If you go when they're collecting the cotton balls you'll see huge carts like bullock carts but tremendously long. And this stuff is all put into bolls, no sheets over it, and the carts creak and creak and creak. Then, when you get to a village, the sound that first strikes you is the pump, pump, pump of the cotton gin . . . And on the way we'd generally sing "Down the Grand Trunk Road" – one of Kipling's, and we'd sing it all the way along . . .'

Mrs Dench was only too familiar with the sound of cotton gins for, in the early 1920s, she and her husband were moved from the mountains to Chichiwatni Road, a railway halt about 130 miles from Lahore. They had two baby girls by now, the first having been born in Tribal Territory and 'therefore a native of Swat'. Men from the prison workshop had made her cot which stood on thick white Peshawar rugs, and husband Will had painted a blue and gold guardian angel on the whitewashed wall above it. The child was christened Gillian 'by the Methodist padre with our salad bowl acting as Font. This rested on a Roman Catholic altar loaned by the Political Agent's wife.'

Now they'd been posted to a police bungalow at the little railway halt which contained also a small bazaar, a resthouse – and a cotton gin. 'I can hear it yet. It beep-

beeped all day and all night. On every side of our oasis (if one could call it that) a sandy plain stretched from horizon to horizon showing scarce a vestige of green except for the sparse foliage of the *kikar* trees planted at exact intervals along the banks of the canal.' The ayah the Denches brought with them took one look at this scenario and departed with tin trunk and bedroll; from then on, Mrs Dench welcomed the occupation of looking after her own children.

She took them for long walks and found 'The lack of roads was a drawback, but one couldn't get lost with the beeping of the gin to guide us home.' The Denches also yearned for bread and a loaf arrived every day on the Karachi Mail from Montgomery, thirty miles distant; but it was so hard and dry they usually settled for *chappattis* with their goat's meat. Several months of this isolation passed before the family made their first visit to Montgomery where '. . . we discovered we were definitely jungli. I had become shy and deprived of small talk and it had taken courage even to enter the Club. The children were jungli too. Gillian hid behind me and Pat wept aloud with disbelief when she saw white faces other than Will's and mine!'

The British used the word 'jungle' loosely to describe any sort of wild, remote, uncultivated area. So Mrs Crookshank, whose husband was Head of the Indian Geological Survey, says that, in the 1920s, you had 'to take everything into the jungle with you' – by which she meant the most rural parts of the Central Provinces. During the cold weather season they were constantly on the move and Mrs Crookshank, who knew nothing about India and its ways, had to 'pick up the housekeeping' as they went along. Their daughter, Helen, was only a year old when they first went on tour and obtaining milk for her was a problem. 'The people wouldn't milk cows for us in many places . . . I had to have almost a herd to get enough to put in our tea and Helen's porridge. A cow would dry up in no time and I'd have to try again with another one.' Their cook bargained for chickens in the villages and she soon learned to ask for a receipt, '. . . perhaps just a bit of paper with a thumbmark on – but otherwise they'd say the Sahib's servant didn't pay for things.'

Later she learned the ropes of camping life and Helen was old enough to play about outside – but always near the tents, 'because you never knew if there were panthers or tigers about'. The afternoons were for resting and in the evenings they went riding, with Helen on her pony. On the days they moved camp they were up with the dawn, but some servants had already gone ahead so that, after journeying about ten miles to a new site, they would find the cook preparing a meal. 'Our stove was usually a pit that the servants dug – shallow, then going deeper, and with earth at the back. They'd find logs to put across the pit and I brought two iron bars to put across them. Then they filled a kerosene tin with water that would rest on the bars so one got some hot water [for a hip bath]. When the tents and everything came in, Ayah and I often put up and made the camp beds together and got things out, such as bedroom shoes and folded mosquito nets and put down our so-called carpets on the bedroom tents' floors.' They had a teak dining table and another for Mr Crookshank's office-work and quite soon each new camp began to look 'quite home-like'.

Nevertheless, after five consecutive months of the camping life, it was grand to return to 'the joys of the flesh pots' at headquarters. And, after living so long 'out of one trunk, half for warm clothes, half for something thin, it's lovely to go back and open up your almirah and see frocks and everything else you want . . . Proper full-size baths! All sorts of joys!'

Among the most joyous-sounding of the junglies' extended tours were those taken by Mrs Florence Meiklejohn in the Goalpara District – through country that was proper jungle. Her husband, Mick, was another forestry officer engaged in surveying areas for planting or felling timber. The Meiklejohns travelled about twelve miles a day on their two elephants, and bedrolls were arranged on her elephant's back upon which she reclined comfortably. The mahout sat in front, whittling twigs to make earrings for his wife or pointing out the wildlife as they plodded through the thick undergrowth. 'We just looked and nobody said a word. I remember his pointing to a deer crouched in a corner. She was very frightened and had her young with her. It was wonderful to see.' Sometimes an elephant '. . . would pull up a tree here and a branch there, but when it pulled a creeper from the top down and I got all the red ants on me it wasn't so good.'

When they reached the next survey site they'd settle in for a week, more or less, but it didn't matter because 'you never knew which day was which, it was all the same.' The only reminder of the outside world was the arrival of a messenger from headquarters bringing mail. He 'came running along with a long stick which had some bells fastened on top – that was to keep animals away. And we'd be sitting in our tents in the evening and we'd hear the bells and say, "Oh there's the dak." We used to call it the dak post. I remember at Christmas once hearing them and we opened the post quickly and there we had a Scotch bun sent from Edinburgh by Mick's mum – right out in the jungle.'

Sometimes they arrived at some old forest bungalow, where she could take a proper bath and change from khaki slacks into a cotton dress for the evening, while the elephants had their baths too. Then came the ritual of teatime. The Meiklejohns were served theirs on the verandah before which stood a row of three or four elephants, 'and in front of each elephant was his mahout feeding him. They were given their tea in the bark of a banana tree, a piece of which would be cut out and rice put into it and wrapped and tied with a strip and given to the elephant who took it and pushed it into his mouth, and then you'd hear those crunching, juicy noises. Then the mahout would get another one ready and the elephant would take it and hold it in its trunk like a child holding a sweet waiting to have the next one. At the end came the very lovely titbit in the very centre of the banana tree which is quite white, round and juicy, and that was the titbit he'd take in his trunk and walk away with.'

Everyone who had to do with elephants grew to love them, but mounting and riding them comfortably was an art to be learned. In the early 1930s, Mrs Cunliffe-Parsons paid a visit to her daughter, married to a Deputy Conservator of Forests, and sent her friend, one Mrs Seal, a highly entertaining account of the 'fearful joy' of her first elephant ride – you might almost call it a voyage – across the River Ganges.

My dear Mrs Seal,
You simply can't think how *desperately* dangerous it is . . . The elephant is nearly up to his eyes in water with his trunk curled upwards to breathe and he has to go so terribly slowly and hardly moves at all! Honestly at one moment my heart was banging so hard I thought I'd drop off my perch.

The elephant suddenly stopped when we were in mid-Ganges! And went slowly sideways – I quite thought the current had got him that time! You see the current is terribly *swift* and simply swirls along underneath one. And the elephant has to steady himself at each step because of the boulders on the bed of the river which are so deep under the water he can't see them. And it is the current racing so *terrifically swiftly* along that makes one quite dizzy. Not even the best swimmer would have a chance in it because of the *rapids* about fifty yards downstream. So one is absolutely at the mercy of the elephant.

One is merely *perched* with legs dangling and with only a short stick [at each corner of the saddle] to hold on to! So one stumble of the elephant and one would be landed *straight* to Kingdom Come. Really, Mrs Seal, it is all very well for the supermen of the Indian Forestry Service and their wives who think nothing of the danger of it, but it *is* jolly well there! And it is all very well to say 'elephants are so surefooted you can always trust an elephant', but surely they are not *infallible*?? And there is always the added risk of a Crocodile. One was sighted about a mile further downstream . . .

I simply marvel to think I am still alive after such an experience. Middle-aged me, who had been jogging along so uneventfully for the past ten years to be suddenly landed in mid-Ganges on the back of an elephant with legs dangling and *nothing* to hold on to but a short stick. Mrs Seal, do you realize how too – tooish it was?! And having done it once, I had to do it a second time. And the second time was, if anything, worse. But it just shows what one *can* do and still *like*!

Mrs Cunliffe-Parsons *liked* it all tremendously. Later, when she'd got accustomed to the elephant's rolling gait on dry land, she and her grandson, little Jimmy, went riding on one together. And, 'Jim's topee fell off and got buried in the scrub and at some order from the mahout, the elephant *searched* for it with his trunk and then handed it back to the mahout over his head!' They climbed up ridges so steep that, at one point, the elephant 'tucked his hind legs under him and *tobogganed* down the other side on his tail-end! And all done so purposefully, slowly and surely it wasn't a bit alarming.' On another jungle jaunt they came upon tiger's pawmarks and 'I simply couldn't believe it was me, standing where a tiger had recently stood. Pre-historic man must have had a hard time of it, but, oh Mrs Seal, think of the *thrills*!'

Her daughter, Lady Champion, shared her zest for the jungli outdoors; 'I *do* think a forester's life is lovely!' she exclaimed, when on tour with her husband, Harry, as he went about measuring tree-girths of sample plots. The

Champions moved from one old forest bungalow to the next in leisurely fashion as the Meiklejohns did. And, 'We lie in bed having our *chotas* [breakfasts] in the morning and see the sun gradually light up the tops of the deodars through the open door opposite and when the beams come through the window at the side and on to the bed, it's time to get up.' While Harry was away measuring, 'I sit sewing under the trees and Jimmy sleeps in the pram and later plays with twigs and flowers at my feet . . . Teatime varies, and then Harry and I go out for a walk together, if he's not working until dark. Then a peaceful time by the fire, reading, bath, dinner and Halma till bed-time.'

Harry's district included that section of the Ganges which Mrs Cunliffe-Parsons had crossed by perilous elephant but which could also be navigated on a very strange vessel indeed. It was, his wife wrote, made up of a *charpoy* with an inflated *sarnai* (inflated buffalo skin) 'tied at each end, one facing one way and one the other. Harry sat on the *charpoy* facing with his feet on the chest of one *sarnai* and I did the same, facing the other way. Dandy [their dog] sat between us. There was just room for us all. Each of the men had another *sarnai* and they lay across them on their tummies with their legs hanging over one side and their heads and arms on the other. They got on each side of us with their *sarnais* facing opposite directions and holding on to ours, they guided us down-river with their legs, in a peculiar sideways motion. In the middle of the river they kept us straight while we were carried by the current. It was just perfect. The sun warm but not hot, the water clear so one could see the bottom.'

Like others of her kind, Lady Champion disliked going to Simla where 'There is nothing whatever to do and you can't get out of it and people look very brass-hatty and unthrilling.' Still, Lady Champion had Harry for escort; Margery Hall, a 'single working lass from Birmingham' who went to stay with friends in Simla, felt that its society was 'only gracious in a formal way and rarely showed warmth to anyone it considered no-one'. Ladies were ranked entirely according to the seniority of their husbands or fathers and, when they went 'to powder their noses after dinner, the senior ladies got the first use of the pristine seats in the loos and left first at the end of every evening'. As an unaccompanied spinster, Margery became 'the only person I know who walked out of every door in that place last'!

But not for long, because, while in Simla, she met and married Henry Hall of the Foreign and Political Service and presumably moved up in the loo queue. To her astonishment, Henry had to get permission from the Viceroy to marry her because he was under thirty, which also meant he got no marriage allowance – and his pay was only about £15 a week. They rationed themselves to a bottle of whisky a month and joined just the one club with the best library. When the second world war started, Henry was called into the army at first, but then sent back into civilian life. This change from 'Political' to 'Military' and back again involved them in more than the usual number of moves – about sixteen in eight years altogether, Mrs Hall reckoned. And by far the worst of them was to Jacobabad, a positive hellhole in the Sind desert about two hundred miles from Quetta.

The year was 1944 – though living conditions in Jacobabad had improved but little during the past fifty years – and the job was for 'two years or as long as Henry's health held out – whichever was shorter'. And what about her own health and that of her three boys under five years old, Mrs Hall wondered? The first of many unpleasant characteristics of the place that struck her was an almost total lack of air and the sickly odour of 'decay, urine and spices' that permeated what little there was. The average temperature of the whole area – and that for *months on end* – was 120 degrees, and, as a result, the town was 'small, dreary, dirty, dusty, very hot and very smelly'. During the long burn of every day its streets were empty, except for diseased donkeys and dogs with fly-covered open wounds. In Jacobabad, Margery soon concluded, 'Everyone and everything was sick.'

Despite the sizzling heat, their ancient bungalow had no refrigerator and was 'cooled' only by electric fans. These moved very slowly and at intervals to fit in with the schedule of trains passing through, as electricity was installed there mainly to supply the signal box. Water was obtained from a well in the garden and brought to the surface by a Persian wheel. It had dozens of little tins attached that filled as they descended into the dark depths and it was moved by a blindfold buffalo that walked round in slow, miserable circles. Owing to the war, the one shop that was supposed to cater for the Halls' needs (as the only resident foreigners) was 'filled mainly with dust'. So they lived on chappattis, rice, lentils, rancid butter, tinned milk (with a taste of rancid coconut about it) and lots of tiny local eggs – about nine out of every dozen being usually putrid.

The kitchen in which this lacklustre diet was prepared was 'a four-walled black hell'; its stove 'a table of mud with two burn-point holes in it and an aperture at the bottom for lighted charcoal'. The bathrooms had the usual holes in the floor 'for water to flow away and snakes to glide in'; there were no flush lavatories of course, and Mrs Hall soon discovered that the servants' earth closets behind the bungalow had long since overflowed and were positively heaving with huge maggots. The smell of the strong disinfectant she ordered to be used liberally everywhere hung in the hot air with the other nauseous odours.

There was no escape from this unlovely spot because it was surrounded by stretches of the same burning sub-desert in every direction. But at welcome sunset, though still dripping with perspiration, the Halls took a little stroll along the canal road – where the local gentry also took the evening air, followed by two bodyguards apiece. This was because they'd made small fortunes growing rice and were liable to be murdered for their money. But they themselves, being foreigners, were quite safe, her husband assured her.

Nevertheless she could not sleep easily when he was away and she was left with her small children in that stifling, smelly old bungalow 'with eleven doors into it that couldn't be locked'. She entitles her memoir 'The Nights were more Terrible than the Days', and in it she describes how she 'moved from one hot wet strip to the next' on her bed and judged the passing hours by the footsteps of the armed sentry who kept guard outside her bedroom door. 'He always stayed until he thought I was asleep, usually about midnight, when I would hear the careful scrunch, scrunch of his boots as he crept off to his own bed.'

One night, half-awake as usual, she heard stealthy rustling sounds very close to her in the bedroom. She switched on the light. A number of 'very large bazaar rats were dabbling their horrid paws in the baby's bottles and food' which she kept on a table, covered with a cloth – which the creatures had removed. When she threw a book at them, they simply stared at her unblinkingly and carried on foraging, and she screamed for help – terrified by a nightmare vision of them closing in on her. The Hindu servants refused to kill them, but a Moslem servant did; she then acquired a couple of cats.

Most of Mrs Hall's energies went into keeping her family safe and well. They had two bad cholera scares (no joke when the nearest British doctor was two hundred miles away) and then she found that practically all the servants had syphilis. Moreover she discovered that her cook, imported from Quetta and nicknamed 'Flash Harry' had set up a flourishing little brothel in one of the servant's quarters at the side gate. He'd furnished it with stolen possessions of theirs and installed a local 'scarlet woman' who had acquired 'much face in the bazaar for having a room in the Memsahib's house'. When Flash Harry was instantly fired, he set up another little establishment down the road on the profits he'd made from hers. His dismissal led to one of the few improvements that occurred during their eighteen months stay in Jacobabad: the hiring of a replacement Goanese cook who could make bread, using a yeast made from a fermentation of raisins, sugar, flour and potatoes.

When their new posting came through, Mrs Hall was so heartily relieved to get away safely and with the family intact that she didn't give a rap when she realized many of her silver spoons had gone missing. She sums up: 'I learned a great deal in the desert, but I hope there will never be anything quite like it again.' And certainly it is amazing that the Halls had to endure, as late as the 1940s, conditions that were more common fifty years before and which (as witnessed by the pathetic little Jacobabad cemetery) many British resident there failed to survive.

Margery Hall's experience was particularly unenviable, and judging by the records, it appears that the most fortunate among the jungli wives were those attached to the Forestry Service. Mrs Meiklejohn is one of several of them to wax nostalgic for that beautiful, lost jungle world she'd known. 'Oh I'd like to be going on tour again with Mick and the elephants,' she concluded. 'Yes, it was lovely. It was all so peaceful and it was a wonderful life really. We had no cares. At least – I had none.' In any case, however carefree, however many the cares, most jungli wives would probably echo the sentiments of Viola Bayley: 'What a wonderfully colourful and varied life we had, certainly compared with the rather humdrum existence that so many of our children's generation are obliged to lead!'

4
After The Kalajuggah

'Before dances the young subalterns used to rush around and borrow things like curtains and heaven knows what else to make something called a *kalajuggah* – a dark place. They all used to have their own to which they used to take their best partners and to which no-one else was allowed to go . . . Oh, it was a great thing, the *kalajuggah* thing!'

Mrs Grace Norie

At more sophisticated functions the 'dark place' could be located behind a potted palm on a secluded verandah or in the Club's attic, but the cavemen tactics used by the suitors were much the same. Subalterns seem to have been specially fond of them and many a girl, enchanted by the romantic, uniformed figure of her 'current scalp', his promises of travel and adventure, committed herself in the intimacy of the *kalajuggah* to a lifetime of 'following the drum'.

Magda Hammersley-Smith was a classic case in point. She went out to India in 1906 and found it was '. . . a romance from morning to night . . . a continual kaleidoscope of colour and movement'. One such excitingly colourful occasion was the Regimental Club Ball of the Jat Lancers in Bareilly. All the officers were in full mess kit, 'The whole building was picked out by tiny oil lamps and lanterns hung in the trees. Beautiful illuminations, it looked like fairyland and there I met [Ralph] again. Between dances one didn't return to a chaperone, but went into one of the cleverly and prettily arranged *kalajuggahs* where you and your partner sat among or under palm branches and chatted. Here we got engaged.'

The times were innocent. When Magda was ready and waiting in her wedding dress a few months later, her brother-in-law 'came hurrying up to my room and said, "Whatever Ralph may do tonight, remember it's all right." And that was all the preparation I had for married life. I wondered what on earth he could mean. I was twenty-three years old!'

She soon discovered what it all meant when she became the wife of a cavalry officer on the North-West Frontier. Every afternoon Ralph 'would take me to look at the horses. We would walk round each horse and admire it from all angles'. When children came along, she tried to enliven the long lunch hours by recounting to her husband 'some clever or amusing thing [they] had done. He would pause a little and say, "Did you see how Melba came up on her haunches into the second chukka?" Not even having heard my nice story about his own daughters!'

Mrs Grace Norie also went travelling up to the isolated North-West Frontier after the romance of the '*kalajuggah* thing'. This was in the earlier days and she made her journey thither in a bullock cart which 'had shutters all round to keep the sun out and also to keep the women private if they wanted . . . You just got into them and slept on a mattress on the floor and did your journeying by night when it would be nice and cool. I think there was a full moon on the night we were leaving and there were these two enormous white bullocks put into the – box on wheels, really. And I always remember the beautiful sight of those white bullocks in the full moonlight taking us along the road to the strange land of the valley of the Doon. We travelled all night and it was a great place for panthers, and I think it might have been quite an adventure, but of course I didn't look upon it as that at the time.'

She learned to take quite a lot in her stride up on the Frontier. The first makeshift piece of furniture in their army bungalow was 'a big wooden packing case with a frill round it to sit on'; her first cook soaked the ham in paraffin instead of champagne – which he'd drunk before her first dinner party began. She grew accustomed to the night sounds of the hyenas and of rats chewing the candles in the dining-room. She learned to sit very quietly up in a tree waiting for the sun to set in order to shoot a leopard. It was, she said, 'a grand life for the men'. But when the day was over, 'you met the same people again and again'. Yet she never saw enough of her husband who was always out at polo or hunting, or with his Ghurkhas, of whom he was 'terribly fond'.

In the strict hierarchies of the Indian Army the Ghurkha regiments were very pukka and their soldiery were great favourites. Mrs Ravenscroft, whose father was a Ghurkha officer, remembers 'what fun it was when they had football matches. One Battalion would play another Battalion, and the wives would come out from the lines with their babies. And Ghurkha babies are the loveliest things you've ever seen, beautiful little creatures with lovely rosy cheeks shining through their bronze skin and glossy bright black heads. The wives were always knitting stocking-tops for their husbands of the most vivid colours you could imagine. I can never think of a football match without seeing those Ghurkha ladies coming along with their balls of wool and their brilliant knitting and those beautiful children being humped along with them.'

However it wasn't all polo and football matches; when the first world war began, the men of the regiment were called to active duty in Europe. 'One day my father came in and said, "It's alright – we're off. We've got our marching orders. They do want us." And the whole station was thrown into uproar . . . men elated and yet worried about their wives, and wives shaking with horror and fear and not quite knowing how bad it was going to be . . . And then the day came for them all to march down, and the wives, daughters and female appendages, we stood watching. There were four battalions to go: the two Garwhal Battalions had their own tune, the 8th Ghurkhas had their regimental march, the 3rd Ghurkhas had their regimental march, and you heard the tunes coming and you saw the men come down and we were all waving to the men as they went. An awful feeling – I can still sometimes see that scene.' Mrs Ravenscroft's great-grandfather and grand-father had been in the same Ghurkha regiment and the third generation – her father – who marched off to that war, was killed in 1917.

During the comparative peace of the 1920s and 1930s, the tradition of being mere 'female appendages' – which was certainly how the military authorities regarded army wives and daughters – continued from one generation to the next. When Mrs B. Bayley, daughter of an army officer, went back to India to rejoin her parents after her education at Home, she took on the voyage 'a blanket chest which had accompanied my grandmother in her regimental travels and the sturdy cabinet trunks used by my mother.'

Her parents lived in a typical military cantonment bungalow – 'single-storied, colour-washed, with flat roofs and a deep verandah'. The master bedrooms had dressing rooms attached which was 'essential when the bearer had to come in and out with polished boots and equipment, laying out uniforms etc'. Later her father was posted to Hyderabad, a big station and a very gay place for a young, unmarried girl. 'There were moonlight picnics to the Moghul tombs of Galconda, their domes like silver bubbles in the silver light. We rode on the old deserted racecourses of Mohl Ali through half-deserted cantonments and across the wide Deccan Plain to ancient crenellated red-sandstone forts.'

Following in the family tradition, she went to stay with an elder brother serving in the Mountain Batteries and there became engaged to a gunner subaltern. She went Home to prepare for her new life in India and, when she returned in 1937, found her fiancé had been posted to a 'field brigade' of Indian artillery in Bangalore. So she went south to join him and they were married among strangers. But this frequently happened in the army and people always rose to the occasion. 'The CO and his wife put me up and arranged the wedding reception, provided a bridesmaid in the shape of a small daughter, gave me away in the garrison church, which had been decorated by the officers' wives. We emerged under a traditional arch of swords and drove to the Colonel's bungalow in an open carriage drawn by a six-horse gun team ridden by officers. In true Anglo-Indian style everyone combined to make it a happy occasion.'

As her husband was under thirty years old there was again no marriage allowance and they had to live 'off the strength', which entailed some economies, such as sharing a bungalow with a batchelor fellow officer. But she was happy in the new life: 'In the early morning, my husband rode or bicycled up to the battery lines while I exercized one of his two polo ponies across the lovely open coun-tryside of Mysore, past villages and tanks, watching the age-old life of the country people.' Guns were still horse-drawn in the 1930s, and horses figured largely in both work and leisure. Her husband '. . . played polo while I rode with the local hunt on a fat mare leased from the battery. We also leased a steady old grey for our dog-cart. The harness, which included a set for a tandem, sported gunner grenades on the blinkers.'

But time tended to drag for her and she made efforts to relieve the even more monotonous and cramped lives of the purdah wives in her husband's battery. She held embroid-ery classes for them, using silks and patterns sent from Home, and she invited her pupils to tea. They were quite fascinated by the inside of a foreigners' bungalow. They pulled her evening dresses from her wardrobe and found that 'most of them had narrow shoulder-straps, so were very indecorous by their decorous standards and occa-sioned some disapproving murmurs as they held them up.' The star attraction, in their eyes, 'was our big double bed.

They bounced on it, talked about it and indulged in peals of laughter, and their children used it as a trampoline. I wished I could join in the jokes, but as *they* were shocked by my dresses, I might have been startled in my turn!'

Army life in the military cantonments of South India was frequently uneventful to the point of boredom, but some found it congenial, particularly in retrospect. Mrs Anna Chitty, married to a captain of the Queen's Own Royal West Kent Regiment, had considerable experience of it when in 1926 she and her husband fetched up in Madras, with which she instantly 'fell in love'.

'Unlike Calcutta, it was still the original eighteenth century city – the buildings exactly as they were in the time of Clive. The quarters [in Fort St George] were all on the first floor with the huge, empty godowns on the ground level, where the merchants stored their goods. The wall was straight, on the sea line, and came to the height of the living floor of our quarters, which rather resembled a Regent's Park terrace trebled in size. The sea, which previously had come up to the walls, was now separated by a wide marine drive, with beautiful flower beds on either side.'

The Chittys' social life was enjoyed in equally spacious and comfortable surroundings. 'The Country Club, the Adyar, was situated by the river, a beautiful white building with wide verandahs where one lunched or dined and the mongooses freely ran around, keeping an eye on any snakes in the vicinity . . . There was a golf course, tennis courts and rowing boats. The club also owned two cabins – ex-railway carriages painted white and black – one for each sex, down on the only safe bit of beach for bathing. A spit of sand some way out made a barrier against unwelcome visits by sharks.'

'. . . Often, after the Saturday night dance at midnight, we used to drive down to the beach and bathe by moonlight. The sea was all phosphorescent, and when we stood up, it looked as if we were covered from head to foot

with diamonds. Sometimes there were a few fishermen out
in their catamarans . . . These consisted of three heavy tree
trunks lashed together with rope, a couple of men with
paddles, clad simply in G-strings. If the elements were
suitable and for a packet of ten cigarettes, they would
willingly take a couple of us out with them, paddle out
beyond the breakers and come racing in. It was a most
exhilarating experience.'

Like the great majority of her kind, Mrs Chitty makes no
mention of the distressing poverty which then existed in
Madras. But Mrs Sarah Davidson, the wife of a sergeant in
the Suffolks, who was quartered in Fort St George a
few years after Mrs Chitty, could not forget that 'though
the city was full of beautiful buildings it was full of poverty
as well. When we strolled down to the bazaar we passed
what was known as Beggars' Pavement, where beggars
were allowed to sit and beg. The sights were heartbreaking.
There was a boy with no arms picking up things with his
toes, another with a head the shape of a coconut, a man
with elephantiasis legs, a blind old woman in rags, two boys
picking lice out of her long matted hair and screaming at
passersby to throw an anna into her coconut-shell. And so
it went on and on, the whole way along the pavement.'

It went on and on in all the large cities of course, and no
single individual could do much about it. And military
wives, particularly those attached to the British army, were
not encouraged to get much involved with the country at
any level. The military structure was hierarchical, conventional and inward-looking, with people constantly moving
from one protocol-ridden circle to another. It was this
moving around, explained Mrs Chitty, which made the
calling-card system so useful. Tin or wooden calling-boxes
hung on every bungalow gatepost: 'Written on the front
side were the rank and names of the owners, with
regimental and other services; and on the back extension,
the words "Not at Home". There was a slit in the lid for the
cards. On leaving the station, p.p.c ("Pour prendre congé"

or "cheerio, I'm off") and on arriving p.p. ("Pour prés-
enter" or "Here I am") cards were popped in the box. The
box was brought in each evening and the cards entered in
the calling book.' In such fashion 'one was kept in touch
with all the comings and goings'.

Kept in touch socially, perhaps, but army wives, in
particular, were certainly treated by the authorities as just
so much 'dust in the balance'. They did not frequent the
messes, they were forbidden to ride on the parade grounds,
they must never let the side down by any conduct
unbecoming – and all the rules were made by men. Said one
who lived among them in the 1930s, but who was not of
them in spirit, 'They wore identical twin-sets with strings of
pearls. Many of them had gone out at eighteen, knocked off
a major and never had to think about much since. They
kept to the rules and most of them were pretty narrow-
minded and conventional. So they didn't take to me much
because I'd been divorced and that shocked 'em a bit.' She
got into trouble too because she overpaid her servants (in
their view), and this started a general demand for higher
wages. And she once asked her Muslim butcher 'a splendid
fellow' to a party – which was not at all correct behaviour
for a 'Proper Army Wife'.

'Proper Army Wives' felt themselves part of their
husbands' regimental 'family' and, as such, were made
welcome by their peer-group wherever they went. According to William, husband of Leonora Starr, author of *The
Colonel's Lady*, a PAW always talked of 'Our subalterns,
Our band, Our regiment, is well informed in all the latest
army shop, knowledgeable in all matters of army routine
and etiquette and given to calling senior officers by their
nicknames.'

Mrs Starr had very little knowledge of these niceties when
she first went out to India on a troopship during the 1930s
and had rapidly to learn an appearance of savoir faire
among other ladies on board who 'knew the meaning of

every bugle-call'. Her early experiences as an officer's wife were typical of the time. On reaching Bombay, she and her husband lunched at the Taj Hotel overlooking the bay where the white-sailed yachts skimmed; at the Army & Navy she bought a basin with a leather top which served 'as a receptacle for sponges and soap until we wanted to wash'. The couple, their two sons and Nanny sailed to Karachi on a coasting steamer and boarded the Quetta Mail at dawn. While crossing the Sind Desert, Leonora was duly surprised to be informed by William that 'the stretches of sandy waste, dotted with tangles of cactus and thorn bushes were called "jungle"'. It was part of the vocabulary of the *quai hais* – one of the two groups to which, she soon discovered, all army personnel in Quetta belonged.

'They called lunch, tiffin, breakfast, *chota hazri*, shooting, *shikar*,' and so on . . . 'Their bungalows were filled with brass elephants, amateurish sketches of Kashmir, carved tables with brass tops, screens carved in minute detail until they were like filigree and, being impervious to any duster, were never clean, and curtains of Indian silk. The other variety clung rather pathetically to every tradition of Home, disguised their cheap furniture (hired from the Government or a dealer in the bazaar) with flowered cretonnes and made their bungalows look as English as they could.'

Another division – of function rather than taste – and noticed by a field officer's wife, was that army bungalow commodes were one of two kinds: 'Cavalry pattern and infantry pattern . . . The cavalry pattern used to be open at the sides of the frame to accommodate an officer wearing spurs. Infantry ones were wooden all round.'

In the Quetta cantonments, life outside the bungalows revolved round the Club, with its usual facilities for tennis, golf, polo, hunting, squash and a library. The ladies were consigned to one large room '. . . like a vast and sombre dungeon lit by two small windows' in Mrs Starr's view, and presumably the nearest the military could get to purdah quarters. The room's liveliest feature was its noticeboard where people moving on or needing cash urgently advertised things for sale: prams, ponies, hats, layettes, goats, decanters, oil-stoves, donkeys, bicycles, rabbits, mowing or sewing machines, mattresses, gramophones, cars, cradles, saucepans and saddlery.

As a newcomer, Leonora was the recipient of quantities 'of bewildering and conflicting information with regard to the amount of charcoal needed by the cook and how much Lux to issue to the dhobi . . . Colonel's ladies initiated me into the mysteries of shopping in the bazaar and engaged a *munshi* to teach me to speak Urdu.' Officers' wives were also expected to help soldiers' wives. One remembered with astonishment how she 'ran little dances and little gramophone things and looked after the families generally. Considering I was only about twenty-five and many of them were older and more experienced, it was rather ridiculous how very much of a "mother" one was expected to be.'

Mrs Starr not only learned some Urdu but passed an examination in it, for which a hundred rupees was paid into her husband's account by a Government which encouraged army wives to learn the language, but not to use it as a basis for making Indian friends. She also learned to hunt – just at the time when officers' ladies were still debating the vexed question of riding astride or side-saddle. Correct horsewomanly gear had not yet been designed for those of the former 'brigade', whose ill-fitting breeches, run up by their local bazaar tailors, caused some scornful merriment among those of the traditional, skirted persuasion.

But it was all rather small beer and Leonora Starr sometimes felt a sense of 'time rushing by with nothing much to show for it . . . We wives of the Staff College [where William worked] spent the hot mornings in sewing, gossiping and drinking tea or lime squashes upon each other's verandahs, and after the siesta most of us watched the polo, played tennis or read the English papers upon the

Club lawn.' Most evenings they 'sallied forth to eat dinners that nearly always consisted of clear soup, fried fish of an anonymous variety, saddle of mutton or roast chicken, "sugar basket" and cheese straws.' Those sugar (or toffee) baskets (or boats) were a special feature of Anglo-Indian cookery. Cooks vied with each other to produce an ever more splendid and fragile concoction of crisp brown spun sugar that looked like a translucent amber dish and was filled with fruit salad. The trick was first to serve the salad and then crack the bowl with a silver spoon and serve that; mistakes occurred – sugar and salad pouring on to cloth or lap at important functions. It was a typical Anglo-Indian 'disaster story'. And the conversation, at most dinners Mrs Starr attended, was equally typical, and as predictable as the menus: 'We talked of horses with the soup and fish, glided into gardening with the entrée, stayed there with the sweet and savoury and when the dessert was handed, broke into reminiscences of some beloved corner of Devon, a Yorkshire moor or a valley in the West Country.'

When not dining out, the Starrs had dinner together on their verandah and made their own conversation, 'sometimes by the light of a gigantic moon, sometimes by candle-light and stars. From the dinner tables of our neighbours other candles winked and flickered at us through the shadows and when they had a Guest Night at one of the regimental messes, the music of their bands floated to us on the breeze, bearing with it a sort of gentle heartache . . . We slept under apricot trees, lulled to sleep by the high music of the crickets that went on night after night all through the hot weather, and were wakened in the mornings by the mercifully distant sound of the regimental bands at their practice or the peculiar strains of bagpipes as played by learning Ghurkhas.'

As the weekend approached, the pulse quickened a little and 'On Friday mornings the roads of the cantonment were gay with fluttering evening dresses borne at arms' length by dhobis who were taking them to be ironed for the Club

dance in the evening. Many a time one could tell that the
Millers were going to be there by seeing Mrs Miller's
flowered chiffon on its way to be freshened up, or notice
that Mrs Hughes' crimson tulle was going to be given yet
another outing.' People asked each other to dinner that
evening, then went along to the Club and danced until
midnight to the strains of one or other of the regimental
bands. Then came supper, which was one of two kinds:
'Sandwiches and lemonade for one rupee per head, served
in the gloomy lounge; or, if your host was rich, you might
troop grandly into the dining room to eat sausage and
mushrooms or bacon and eggs for two rupees a head.
Generals, brigadiers and senior politicals were always
given the two-rupee supper.' It took most of Saturday to
recover from that, and, on Sunday mornings after church,
people gathered again on the Club Lawn, 'all dressed up in
our best while one of the regimental bands played Gilbert
and Sullivan'. And then they all went to their bungalows to
prepare for another week of much the same again.

'Affairs went on in all the stations and lots of gossip about
them,' recorded one army wife of similar vintage. It was,
she thought, mainly because the women were bored stiff.
'After about eleven in the morning they had simply nothing
to do and were treated rather like royalty – with servants to
pander to their every whim.' Confessed another, 'We had
nothing to do but enjoy life, you see. It sounds dreadful
now. But there it was!' And so it was – as Leonora Starr
summed it up – 'A lazy, easy, pleasant life, but inclined to
make one sluggish in mind and character.'

Mrs Iris Portal was one determined not to sink into
sluggishness, even though she followed the conventional
pattern of marrying a cavalry officer who was one of her
father's ADCs. She had 'had a love affair with India since
childhood' and, prior to marriage, had learned to speak
fluent Urdu like her mother. As the elder daughter of Sir
Montagu Butler, she had enjoyed several Simla 'seasons'.

One of her amusing memories from that 'awfully giddy time was watching a chorus of maharajahs' wives singing a popular chorus of the period: "I'm tickled to death I'm single, I'm tickled to death I'm free."'

After her marriage, Mrs Portal went to live 'in an appalling little cantonment at Poona' as an ordinary captain's wife. For compensation there were always the horses, which she'd adored since the time when, as a small child, she'd been taken out to tea in Simla riding very high indeed on a big steed called By Chance. So she rode a lot, 'went hunting those poor wretched jackals', and followed up her enthusiasm for Indian history, first developed among the ruins of Old Delhi, by studying the Mahrattas who once ruled the region around Poona.

After a while her husband was posted to Meerut, a cavalry brigade centre and an even horsier place. Officers' wives there were supposed 'to watch their husbands banging round on the polo ground every single bloomin' afternoon', while they chatted about 'the high cost of soda water and how much to pay the bearer'. That sort of thing bored and irritated her, but as the wife of a junior officer, she was unable to put her knowledge of the country and its customs to much constructive use. Her role was 'to pay, pack and follow and that I did'. Though distanced from the country and dismayed by her companions' lack of understanding and sympathy for it, 'the haunted, spiritual quality of India, the richness of its history still came through' to her. She bore her second daughter in a hospital run by Minto nurses in Delhi where some British people had been besieged during the Mutiny. And it seemed 'extraordinarily romantic to be stuck up there listening to the peacocks calling and thinking about what happened there not so very long before.'

In due course, her husband was promoted to the command of the Governor's Bodyguard in Bombay which meant he 'had his own little kingdom with two troops of horses'. And the high point of their year was the feast of

Dessehra '. . . the ten days that celebrate the victory of Rama over the demon Ravana, symbolic of the victory of good over evil'. At its finale, 'All weapons of war were garlanded – sword, rifle, shot gun, service revolver. The horses came up from the stables with roses on their headstalls and marigolds round their fetlocks and coloured shawls on their backs.'

The Bodyguard's Family Lines became her little kingdom with which no superior memsahib could interfere. Her first concern was for the mostly Moslem wives '. . . sweet women, but dreadfully confined in little brick places and so unhealthy'. She persuaded the Governor's wife to get their quarters improved and '. . . got hold of a small van with a curtain round it and a man to drive. And we used to push the ladies inside, shut the doors and drive right into the country where I made them walk out and about a bit in the sun, among a grove of trees. Their children began to play for the first time and their health improved a little.'

She discovered that the women customarily delivered their babies 'in the squalid back rooms of their tiny habitations on piles of dirty rags' – which resulted in much infection and disease. She raised funds to employ a trained midwife for them and later had them sent to a wing of Government House hospital. It was true 'some British took the view that one needn't bother about Indian women because they were in purdah, but if you looked, you couldn't help but see the oppressiveness of it in some respects.'

Mrs Portal's familiarity with the language and customs of the country meant that the Governor's wife used often 'to whistle her up' to oil the conversational wheels with important Indian visitors. And she was also expected to act as one of the 'unpaid, female ADCs after dinner, with the duty of settling Her Excellency on a sofa and leading up ladies to talk to her'. So, when one's husband attained a certain rank, the rituals of the red carpet came within reach of some officers' wives and had to be duly followed. But women married to soldiers and NCOs (and they were termed 'women', not 'ladies') never got within whistling distance of a single red carpet however many years they spent in India.

Mrs Annie Lee, recently married to Corporal Lee, bandsman, sailed for India in 1909 on a troopship which had 'open decks with sleeping places for all women and children' while the men had to sling their hammocks somewhere else. Measles broke out during the voyage so she spent her first weeks in India confined to barracks quarantine. She was then packed off to Dalhousie inside a *dhoolie* through which monsoonal rains poured, swamping her bedroll and ruining her best hat inside its box.

They had to live in tents at first and were issued with two string beds, two mattress-cases and 'so many pounds of *kya* – a stuff like coconut matting . . . And when you get it – take it outside and get little boys to toss it up and beat it with a cane or something till they loosen it all up and you stuff that into your mattress cases.' There were no shops in the vicinity of the camp, but meat and vegetable wallahs came round each day and 'you got regular rations of sugar, flour etc, bread from the Government Bakery . . . and a matey brought round pats of butter from the military dairy'. As a mere wife, she got no rations of her own: 'All the rations you got were your husband's.' She used to cook supper outside the tent on an oil stove (while beating away swarms of insects) and serve it to her husband when he'd finished playing at the officers' mess each evening. It was pretty tough on a young woman, but 'you got used to it. You get used to anything in time, if you have to'. That was bred-in-the-bone philosophy for one whose father had served in the Boer War and whose husband had been 'a boy-soldier from the age of nine when he first learned to play the cornet'.

After a time the Lees were posted to Peshawar, where the nearby frontier was, as usual, troublesome. Soldiering there 'was hard going'; discipline was strict and the native town was out of bounds for British women who were only allowed to go to the Government bazaar and buy from Indians licensed to sell to the military. 'There were no doors on the barracks, just very bleak places in the hills, rifles in racks and soldiers on guard every night.' Family living quarters certainly weren't palatial: 'No running water or anything like that, the bathroom just rough brick with white-washed walls and an iron frame to hold an enamel basin.'

She still did her own cooking because she was 'fussy' and didn't trust Indians to do the job. She used a little Rippingdale stove in the corner of the cookhouse which also contained a boiler for heating water. It was fired with wood cut from the neighbouring forests which was the only source of heat during the severe winters. 'A great pile of wood was put in the back of your quarters once a month and Pathan tribesmen – large, wonderful-looking men from the hills with axes over their shoulders' – came to chop it up. Barrack fireplaces were just hollows set against a wall: 'They always improvised for us.'

Annie produced three children during her years in India and when she was pregnant the sergeant in charge of hiring servants used to say, ' "Alright, Mother Lee, you've got to have a cook now. I'll get you a good one." ' So she was spared, for a while, the heat and inconvenience of the communal cookhouse. She had her babies in the military hospital where 'all you had was the midwife and she was often Eurasian'. Once out of hospital she brought up her own children without the help of ayahs who, in her view, were expensive and untrustworthy. There was nowhere to buy clothes for them, so she purchased material from the 'cotton wallah' and made them up herself.

Topee-wearing was obligatory for all white children in India at that time and an army child seen without one could be reported to the Orderly Room. The youngsters love to run wild in the nearby hills and catch moths, big ones, 'like white birds' which they pinned round their

topees in lieu of badges. There wasn't much else in the way
of entertainment for them or their mother, except putting
the same old records on His Majesty's Voice gramophone
and loyally going to listen to the band in which father
played.

During one of her earlier summers in the barracks, Mrs
Lee was taken on as a temporary lady's maid to the wife of the
District Commissioner – a rather unusual arrangement. She
'had a lovely time', even though the Commissioner's lady,
who hadn't been married long, was 'rather a snob'. 'I used to
stand brushing her hair for ages and all that sort of thing,'
which was closer contact than she usually had with high-
ranking ICS wives, or their military equivalents. 'They were
very snobbish in the army, you see, very snobbish.' (And it
was not only the officers' wives: sergeants' wives did not mix
socially with those 'below' them.)

The Colonel's Lady of the Lees' regiment, who rode atop
a big four-in-hand chaise with her sons, would come
dutifully to the door to enquire after Mrs Lee's children
when they were ill with whooping cough or bronchitis. 'But
it was funny, she'd say, "I won't come in. I've never had
whooping cough in my life."' Nor did she come in until her
boys caught the disease when she rushed to Annie for
advice on how to nurse them! Nevertheless she was, in Mrs
Lee's opinion, 'a lovely lady', and the regiment's officers
'were all gentlemen, I will say that'.

By the time Sarah Davidson went to India in the late 1920s
conditions for the 'other ranks' seem to have improved.
Before they went to Madras, the Davidsons were stationed
at Trimmergarry, near Secunderabad where, she testifies,
'We had the most lovely quarters provided for us. In fact
wherever we went we always had nice married quarters.'
Their home was surrounded by 'lovely green palms,
banyan and mango trees to keep it cool and with a lovely
long verandah. Around the floor inside the rooms it was
painted white so any crawling insect could be seen. In each

room were large fans fixed to the ceiling and the table legs stood in round tins of water to keep ants from the food. If you dropped a crumb you could see it being taken away by swarms of sugar ants.'

An army lorry picked up her children about seven every morning and took them to the army school, returning them home before eleven o'clock. It was a short school day, 'But they got on very well indeed as I think travelling and seeing how people live in different countries is an education in itself.'

Sarah Davidson, like Annie Lee, was quite determined to make the best of things rather than 'packing up and going back home after a few months, like some of the wives did'. For her, the everyday scenes of Indian life itself provided an endless source of pleasure and interest. 'We loved to stroll down the bazaar in the evening. All along outside of their quarters, the silk wallahs squatted cross-legged on the ground along with other wallahs displaying their wares such as soft slippers, sandals, pearls and beads and tin toys, razors, scents and bright-coloured sweets etc. Outside his hut would sit a *derzie* [tailor] on an old durrie with an old machine sewing away. Then a very thin Sikh with a long beard wearing a dazzling white long tunic and turban and with his hand scales was weighing the rice, lentils, flour, sugar, curry powder from baskets that stood on wooden planks. There was the betel leaf shop, toddy shop and stalls where ghee and cooking oil were sold, and old natives smoking their hubble-bubble pipes.

'All along the bazaar the coolie boys would be shouting out to carry your goods for you. The wallahs would give you so many annas discount in the rupee. Further along, the Parsee quarter, where bejewelled, gorgeously attired women sat on low stools padded with cushions and in the windows and on the balconies over curious little shops where betel nuts and such like were sold. As the darkness came on, the tom-toms were beating out music and native girls covered in jewels, rings and bangles singing love-songs and dancing, swaying their bodies and tapering their arms and doing slow motions of enchantingment [sic], their olive skins reflecting in large mirrors, and passersby threw them annas. There was always the bazaar smell of ghee, of strange spices, pipe smoke and romantic perfumes wherever you strolled along.'

Exotic perfumes and the hint of romance, colour, liveliness and 'enchantingment' – Sarah Davidson remembers it all with nostalgia in her old age. And Leonora Starr, the Colonel's Lady who remained at a further remove from the Indian scene, still felt that same sense of wonderment, strangeness and beauty lost which she expresses in these wistful verses:

After the Journey

I have seen the flocks of red and emerald parrots
Wheeling, screaming in the low green Indian plains;
And the high snows in the lonely mountain passes,
The white snows in the silent mountain passes,
And the sullen, ceaseless pouring of the rains.

I have heard the palms on golden-sanded beaches
Sending the surf's low song back to the seas;
I have seen the peacocks dancing in the jungles,
Their old fantastic dances in the jungles
Where creepers hang in curtains from the trees.

I have loved the old palaces of the Moghuls,
The emptiness and silence of their courts,
And the long-deserted citadels of Delhi –
Dead towns that once were capitals of Delhi;
And grassy walls of the old sleeping forts.

I shall dream of rose-red cities in the sunshine
(Sitting by the fire, some rainy English night),
And of Akbar's milestones, sentries on his highway –
Great Akbar's milestones, marking still his highway
Where Moghul armies once rode out to fight.

5
Untold Good

'These Mission Hospitals do untold good in
India and you find them everywhere in the
most benighted regions, with just a few,
perhaps two or three, wonderful men and
women who spend their lives ministering to
the sick.'

Lady Reading, Vicereine, 1921–5

The amount of simple, straightforward good in the form of
ministering to the sick that was accomplished by British
women living in India during this period has not yet
received the recognition it deserves. Library and missionary archives contain numerous accounts by and about
female doctors and nurses, attached to both missionary and
secular institutions of every conceivable kind and in all
parts of the country. Most of them went out to India when
they were quite young and found such a crying need for
their professional services that they remained for many
years leading dedicated, hardworking, often isolated lives
that have remained 'untold'.

Lady Reading, who encouraged greater public recognition of their worth, also did what she could herself. During
her first stay in Simla she visited the native hospital where
she saw 'Little children so frail, so rickety . . . All of them
with their lovely dark eyes pencilled round with *kohl*. The
stories I heard were terrible, the scenes I saw. Such
neglect and poverty – above all such superstition, such
graft. I went home miserable, for it seems almost impossible to fight it. I feel my work in India ought to be directed
in that channel'.

With that decision Lady Reading was following an

honourable line of Vicereines – Ladies Dufferin, Minto, Hardinge – who put considerable effort into trying to alleviate sickness and disease among the Indian poor, especially women. For they, and some of their contemporaries, were particularly appalled at the amount of abnormality and infection associated with pregnancy and the high mortality rate of babies and mothers – particularly of girls scarce out of childhood themselves.

At that time, Indian doctors were all male and were forbidden by purdah restrictions from attending female patients suffering various gynaecological problems about which most of them were woefully ignorant anyway. This left women in labour at the mercy of the local *dai* (midwife), usually an elderly woman with no medical training who relied on traditional lore passed down from her maternal forebears. Her typical 'tools of the trade', carried in an old cloth bag, have been described as 'a rubber enema syringe, lumps of dirty cotton wool, bottles with no labels, a vaseline jar without a top, bundles of country drugs, a loose, dirty hank of surgical silk wound round the mess' which was never sterilized and dumped on the mud floors of various peasant dwellings.

The book which did most to focus public attention on the sufferings caused by the custom of child marriage that resulted in early and frequent pregnancies was Katherine Mayo's *Mother India*, first published in 1927. Mrs Mayo described in graphic, unsparing detail the full horrors of girls under eleven who were raped and ravaged by their adult husbands, of women not yet twenty who were 'internal wrecks', of the prevalence of infant mortality and venereal disease. Even missionaries (who knew most about such matters at first hand) had glossed over things for years, she claimed, while official decorum allied to a reluctance to offend high-class Indian men had prevented earlier disclosures by the Government. Now, public sympathy and anger was aroused, and the book directly inspired several British women to go to India to try and improve the situation.

One of them was Dr Eileen Morris, who qualified from University College, London in 1925 and then discovered (as did other professional women of her generation) that, because of the amount of discrimination against her sex, she was unable to obtain a good job. When she read Mayo's book she realized that 'more work than I could ever hope to finish' awaited her in India. She first went out at her own expense and later joined the members of the St Stephen's Community in Delhi, which was rather special on two counts. Firstly because it was a community of all women workers founded in the nineteenth century, secondly because it was actually situated in the very heart of Old Delhi.

So central was the Community house, incidentally, that it was commandeered for the accommodation of Indian royalty during the durbars of 1903 and 1911. On the latter occasion, it was taken by the Maharajah of Trevancore and his extensive entourage, electricity was installed for him and his rent helped to support the Community's endeavours for a while. St Stephen's hospital, where Dr Morris worked, already had a long and honourable history. It was started as a medical dispensary in a hired room on the crowded Chandri Chowk in 1876 and was opened by Lady Dufferin in 1885 – the first hospital in Delhi run by women for women.

By 1929, when Dr Morris joined the staff, there was a two-storey block of wards with an operating theatre with 'cottage wards' attached where patients' families could stay and a nursery for abandoned or orphaned babies. The maternity ward was always full. Women who'd never left their homes before became in-patients suffering from illnesses such as anaemia or osteomalacia – a softening of the pelvis caused by a deficiency of light and air since early childhood. Women from the outlying valleys were carried to the hospital on charpoys, '. . . in a ghastly state, having been mauled about by the local *dai* . . . We often had to operate and midwifery was very challenging then. Often the cases had gone too far before they were brought to us. It made an enormous difference to the survival rate of patients when penicillin came into general use.'

The hospital worked 'rather on the Robin Hood principle' – meaning that wealthy families were charged high fees, poor villagers hardly anything. The Community Sisters lived very frugally together and, Dr Morris said, 'When I first joined we had to wear grey frocks for winter and white in summer and we were known as the "grey ladies".' They were expected to follow 'quite a strict rule of life with services held during every day'. Bible women went round the wards with texts and Christian literature was laid out in the waiting rooms. Dr Morris found however (as did many other medical missionaries) that she 'was simply too hard-pressed with work' to do much evangelizing.

It was a rigorous life, but brought its own rewards. The hospital was the first in Delhi to open a 'clinic for well babies' and a pre-natal clinic that was 'soon bursting at the seams'. And it was very satisfying to see Indian girls becoming excellent trained nurses – and a few aspiring to become doctors. 'Looking back on it,' said Dr Morris at the age of ninety-two, 'I'm very glad indeed I spent my life as I did.'

The women of St Stephen's Community were regarded by the British community with rather more respect, even admiration, than many of their kind. This was partly, perhaps, because of their almost nunlike life style and also because their dedicated, selfless work was manifestly going on near at hand and for all to see. This in itself was quite unusual for, ever since the Mutiny, it had been Government policy not to interfere with the religious beliefs of the people; any form of Christian proselytizing was therefore regarded with suspicion by the authorities for fear it might provoke trouble.

In consequence, missionaries were usually kept away from the large population centres and obliged to work in rural areas and often among 'the tribals'. These groups were neither Hindu nor Moslem, and Christian converts among them did not face social ostracism, as members of the main religions often did. Their more flexible approach to spiritual matters meant 'there were always mass movements of tribals into Christianity at time of famine', as one missionary remarked – a state of affairs reminiscent of the 'rice-Christians' of nineteenth-century China.

On the whole, therefore, missionaries were isolated from the mainstreams of British society – which had little contact with or sympathy for their work. Missionaries didn't usually smoke, drink, dance or hunt; they travelled second or even third class in the trains; they 'didn't come from much of a background'; and their efforts to convert Indians to Christianity were considered 'a thorough waste of time' by the secular majority. 'I soon discovered that we were regarded as the lowest form of animal life in the district', remarked one lady missionary recently arrived in Bengal.

For the most part, missionaries managed successfully to ignore their lack of status; they often lived in close-knit communities of like-minded people and could usually count on the support of their own families at least. Typically, British female medical missionaries in India came from some sort of clerical background, had been active in Student Christian Movements and married missionaries or clerics – if they married at all.

Dr Honor Wilkins was a case in point. Her family was connected with the church; she'd been inspired by listening to the famous missionaries, Miss French and Miss Cable, talking about their work in China; she met her future husband, Gordon, 'at a squash in connection with the Baptist Missionary Society in Philarmonic Hall, London'. She became a qualified doctor in 1930 and gained some practical experience in surgery before embarking on a career as a medical missionary. She was called before a Selection Committee of Baptist Missionaries – 'an enormous table with lots of elderly men and all rather imposing and I felt very small and very frightened'. But she got through all right and the newly-wed Wilkins went to India for their first five-year term in 1932.

Honor Wilkins' first real challenge came when she was called to help deliver the baby of a local ranee – an important event, for the raja had been waiting nine years for a son and heir. She'd had little actual experience of midwifery then and it was a difficult forceps case; her only help 'was the hand of the local Indian doctor coming through a gap in the purdah curtain to hold the patient's pulse.' The labour was long; outside, above the women's screams, she heard the hubbub of the raja's retinue waiting impatiently for news of the birth. Eventually it came – 'a boy, thank goodness!' While the mother nearly bled to death, riotous rejoicing and displays of fireworks began throughout the palace. Luckily both mother and baby survived and, at his naming ceremony, she, the guest of honour, was presented with a little gold ring. From then on, Honor's standing rose and the sick came from afar to seek her medical help.

After two years both the Wilkins were invalided home and, while there, took extra medical qualifications – Honor in midwifery, her husband in tropical diseases. Their instructions, on returning to India, were to start a new hospital, to be called the Moorshead Memorial Hospital in the Kond Hills of central Orissa. 'Starting' was truly from scratch, beginning with the selection of a suitable site in an area of uncultivated land covered with prickly date bushes. Armed only with a box sextant, T-square, drawing board and compass, Gordon Wilkins 'drew a plan on linen which was copied on to ferrocyanide blueprints'.

Building contractors did not exist in the region and the missionaries had simply to plan and supervise the work themselves. To lay the foundations, stones were brought from the hills on bullock carts and broken with hammers by the local women. Kilns were made in which stacks of mud bricks were fired and sand was carted from a nearby river bed. 'We had to burn our own stones of quicklime which was mixed with charcoal from the forests and burnt in a kiln'. Lime and sand mixed with brick dust was ground in a mortar mill – a heavy stone dragged in a circular trench by a yoke of oxen.

Doors and window-frames were made by local carpenters from durable hardwoods cut in the nearby forest and some American Baptists from their missions' industrial school came along to help make a tube well. After months of work involving much trial and error, a water tower was constructed with a five hundred gallon tank on top and pipes leading to the new buildings. When Honor Wilkins ceremonially turned on the first tap, 'People came from miles around to see water flowing from it.'

The Wilkins had now not only precious water but a small supply of ice made in a kerosene-operated refrigerator called an 'Icy Ball'. Explained Gordon Wilkins, 'This apparatus consisted of two large metal balls connected by an arching pipe. The hot ball was heated by a kerosene stove for an hour and a half while the cool ball was immersed in a tub of water. By this means, fluid in the hot ball was driven over to the cold and, when the cold one was placed in the cabinet, the process was reversed, causing cooling.'

The first hospital buildings were separate bungalows containing whitewashed wards, and a row of sheds, one used as a laboratory with a work bench made from packing cases. Honor's top priority was to open a women's clinic in one of the bungalows; it proved instantly popular, for patients preferred to be treated by one of their own sex. Hearing of its existence, wealthy Hindu ladies came from miles around in hope of cure and Honor had to be careful 'not to give them preference over the local hill women'. She had to cope in the one clinic with all her patients – 'the infertile, the too fertile, anaemic women, children with malnutrition . . . We had to treat syphilis and gonorrhoea as a background to pregnancies, hookworm disease, bear maulings gone septic, everything mixed up, so it was a general all-purpose clinic, mine.'

They were always short of medical supplies, especially vitamins, senna pods, iron tablets and calcium. Milk was in short supply too because the local people used what they had to rear calves for ploughing. So Honor hadn't enough for her own two children, much less for the abandoned babies that soon accumulated there – as on the steps of every mission hospital. So they built a cowhouse 'with a thatched roof, a proper stone floor, a drainage channel and stalls of hardwood jungle timber'.

Honor took to dairying with enthusiasm. She bought three cows to start off with 'that were tethered in the stalls on chains made by the local blacksmith' and she began a proper pedigree book for them. She learned how to syringe their hoofs to prevent maggots and once had to deal with an outbreak of foot-and-mouth disease. She then got a small government grant which enabled them to fence in an area of land for the growing of elephant and guinea grass, lucerne and soya beans for feed.

When her herd was six strong, 'I bought the best little bull, a scrub bull called Billy Black, a poor hill specimen really but it was all I had. I did the best I could and used to sell the calves at a good profit because I looked after them well.' The Viceroy, Lord Linlithgow, who was keen on agricultural projects, heard about their little enterprise and decided they needed a bigger and better bull, so he sent up 'a large white Hariana'. 'But my poor little hill cows were so small and weak that when they saw this enormous bull coming they lay flat down and shivered, and in over two years he was up there he didn't produce one calf.' But he *did* have to have special food and a special keeper – so that viceregal bull was rather a mistake. Still, there was always plenty of good fresh milk for the mission, although it was difficult to persuade the local mothers to give it to their own young.

The Wilkins spent sixteen years in their self-built hospital. Many improvements were made – such as mosquito-screening in the wards, septic tanks, an addition to the always over-crowded women's clinic. There was no electricity supply, but they developed their own 'shadow-less operating light'. It consisted of a Petromax paraffin lamp hung inside two circles of iron rods to which were fixed twenty shaving mirrors bought in the local bazaar. By its bright light, Gordon performed many operations at night, while his wife helped with the anaesthetics.

The Wilkins also did research to try and improve the nutritional standards of the tribal Konds, who were often reduced to eating cakes of flour made from ground mango kernels during the hot weather 'hungry season'. By now, the people's earlier suspicions of the missionaries' endeav-ours had been dispelled to such an extent that some families took up permanent residence in the hospital compound. These included a cowherd, a laundry woman who ironed sheets with a charcoal-heated iron, a gardener who pumped water from the tank every day and a cook 'who was a great character and wrote his own version of Mrs Beeton's in Kiu' – his native tongue. The doctors Wilkins stayed in Orissa during the strains and shortages of the war years and eventually, reluctantly left India for good in 1951. They took little with them in the way of tangible assets, but Honor still wore on her finger the little gold ring given her by the grateful ranee.

There were a considerable number of missionaries in Bihar, Orissa and Bengal and, naturally, the mainspring and inspiration of their work was Christianity. But the emphasis of missionary endeavour had changed from the direct, nineteenth-century aim of 'converting the natives' to one of providing examples of selfless service, of 'bearing witness to the Christian truth', that would make an impact on the people and lead, hopefully, to their conver-sion.

One remarkable woman who devoted her life to this principle and whose pioneering achievements in the medical mission field were quite outstanding was Dr Ida Scudder. She was born into a large family of American missionaries, many of whom spent their entire lives in India – her grandfather being the first American medical missionary to go there. After qualifying as a doctor, she returned to Vellore in South India where her parents had their mission. And, as early as 1902, she achieved the first of her many ambitions – to open a proper hospital for Indian women.

The main building was a red-brick rectangle 'built about a sunken garden and completely surrounded by shady verandahs'. There was a spotless operating theatre with rows of shining surgical instruments and wards of neat white beds – all of this financed by philanthropists unable to resist Ida's fervent powers of persuasion. But these standards of western hygiene were hard to maintain: 'A patient would spit betel juice on floor and walls, wipe her dirty hands on wall or sheet. She'd wear her sheet as she got out of bed, walk round in her bare feet, get back to bed without cleaning them. The floor was the easiest place to throw rubbish. Members of the family, permitted to accompany the patients to hospital in order to satisfy numerous caste dietary requirements, were constantly getting underfoot with their sleeping mats and cooking equipment.' In these conditions, it was difficult to teach inexperienced young Indian women the rules of Western medical practice. 'One might prepare a sterile douche, only to see a hand put in to test its warmth. Conditioned to use only the right hand for most activities, the girls took months to learn to pass things with both hands in the operating room.'

Only a few of the people requiring medical care were able to come to the hospital, so Dr Ida set up what was, for those days, a highly original scheme – a mobile dispensary. In 1909 she acquired her first car, a French Peugeot '. . . high

and open with a folding top, wire-spoked wheels . . . Its
steering wheel rose straight up from the footboard and the
vibrations from the engine were so violent that the driver's
hands seemed at times to shiver with ague'. Nothing like it
had been seen in Vellore before and at first it caused great
excitement.

As the car was small 'only a few drugs could be taken,
powders of all kinds were put in bags and hung along the
windshield. Small bottles of iodine and other medicines
were arranged in long boxes. White uniform swathed in a
duster, topee securely anchored by a long veil, Ida sat in
front with the driver, with Salomi [her Indian assistant]
and a religious teacher behind.' At first, 'it was laughable –
and heartrending – to see the strings of people all along the
way holding up a vast assortment of receptacles: coconut
shells, inkwells, tin lamps, flower vases, bottles' to receive
the foreign doctor's medicines.

This meant stopping constantly and Dr Ida soon
arranged instead to halt each week at specified locations.
As the car approached, 'Ten to fifty people might be
waiting. Hearing the rattle of the engine and the blasts of
the horn . . . others would drop their work and come
running across the fields. They came with every sort of
ailment and disease – dysentery, blindness, scabies, lame-
ness, abscesses, broken bones, foreign objects in their ears
and noses, elephantiasis, leprosy, tumours.'

It was very evident that one gallant doctor in one
small Peugeot could not hope to cure the enormous
medical needs of the district and that more people must
be trained for the work. Eventually Ida, who was an
extremely effective persuader, obtained sufficient funds to
start a missionary medical school for women with herself
as principal. It was opened in 1918 with the blessing of
the Governor of Madras – just the second of its kind in
the country. Its first courses, for 'Apothecary and sub-
Assistant Surgeons only' were attended by fourteen
students and there was considerable scepticism among

British and Indian male doctors that any of them would succeed.

Dr Ida's students accompanied her on ward rounds, assisted in the dispensary, observed operations. She taught them physiology and anatomy: 'Dissection had to be practiced on an occasional cadaver from the Vellore jail. There were only one or two books, one microscope, one skeleton. But Ida made full and graphic use of the last. She equipped it with all appurtenances, using red ribbons for arteries, blue for veins, yellow for nerves; stitched muscles which would flex when strings were pulled; covered it with pale-covered cloth simulating skin. The girls in return did some costuming of their own, dressing the skeleton in fancy clothes and placing it in various staff bedrooms.' The fun was occasional; the hard work continuous, but it paid off. All fourteen of Dr Ida's student 'lambs' passed their first stiff examination set by the Madras Medical Department. A year later, Dr Scudder herself was awarded the Kaisar-i-Hind gold medal first class for 'public service in India'.

The moving force in Dr Scudder's life till then and for the next twenty years she spent in India was her devout Christianity, and she always sought to combine gospel teaching with her medical work. But not all qualified female doctors felt as she did; some preferred to join mission hospitals in a secular capacity – attracted often by the opportunity to use their professional skills to the full without the interference and prejudice of the male medical establishment.

One of these was Dr Claire Thomson whose previous medical experience had been in New Zealand. Lacking the total commitment of the missionary, she went to India at her own expense in the late 1930s to join a community of nursing sisters in Bihar as a 'lay doctor'. The mission was located at Itki, a small town fourteen miles from Ranchi, where 'the social occasion of the day' was the arrival of the train. Dr Thomson lived in a separate bungalow in the mission compound and devoted her considerable energies to helping in their leprosy clinic, performing operations in their hospital and attending difficult cases with the sisters. On arrival, she was fairly appalled by some of the drastic 'cures' practised by local healers – such as cutting any unexpected lump from the body with a hot sickle, pouring goat's milk or onion juice into sore eyes and encouraging female relatives to stamp on the belly of a woman whose labour was prolonged.

The people usually tried such traditional remedies first and only came to the mission when all else had failed. Among the common complaints that did not respond to local treatment were bowel infections and Dr Thomson discovered her patients frequently had hookworm or roundworm eggs in their stools. 'So we decided to get some patients to bring up specimens. As containers were needed, we asked the Club to give some old cigarette tins. We got ten, and handed them out to patients, but very few were returned to us as, in that part of the country, tins were a very valuable commodity. One day an excited woman said to me, "You gave my boy some medicine and a serpent came out. I want to see if I have serpents too". When the doctor explained that there were no containers left for the woman to carry her specimen in, she replied, "Oh that's all right, I'll fasten it in a leaf and bring it to you".' It was a problem solved: from then on 'all patients brought their specimens inside shiny green leaves and fastened, like their plates, with pieces of grass or tiny twigs.'

There were few roads in the countryside surrounding the mission; peasants lived in clusters of small houses in the middle of waterlogged paddy fields that were connected by muddy raised paths too narrow for even a bicycle. When men arrived on Dr Thomson's verandah asking for help with a difficult birth, she would ask how many rivers away they lived and how deep the rivers were. And they'd answer by indicating the height of water on their own bodies. But however deep that answer, she and one sister used to sally forth.

'We gave the midwifery bag and the storm lanterns to the men and started to follow them across the rice fields. These were flooded while the rice was growing, but very dry after the harvest. When we got near the village we looked to see if there was a group of men sitting outside any of the houses. If so, we knew the baby hadn't yet been born. The room chosen for the delivery was usually the worst in the house, often where the grain was stored. It was always dark and when our eyes became adjusted to the poor light we saw the mother lying on the ground in one corner and the rest of the space taken up by onlookers and huge baskets of grain. The first thing we did was to ask all but about six of the women to go outside, and then drove out the hens that were clucking round. The mother was often in a bad way and had probably been in labour for several days because otherwise it wouldn't have been worthwhile sending for us.' In such cases delivery was usually by forceps, and afterwards, before leaving, Dr Thomson made sure the mother had 'a strong brew of very sweet tea' made with supplies she carried in her bag for the purpose.

One day two men arrived on the doctor's verandah wanting to buy a teat, which she took as an encouraging sign of progress. 'Now, I thought, I can give them some antenatal teaching, and I started off at full tilt. After talking for a bit, my Indian assistant broke in, "But doctor, they want the teat for the cow's child!"'

Dr Thomson went to the Itki mission in the 1930s and, like the Wilkins, just gritted her teeth and carried on throughout the war years. She was then working in four district hospitals around Ranchi, one of which, at Kamdara, was regularly cut off by floods for about three months at a stretch during the monsoon season. Occasionally, runners brought letters and newspapers across the waters on hollowed-out tree trunks and 'every two weeks coolies carried laundry boxes to the nearest mission station'. The rest of the hospital staff was Indian, and Claire Thomson confesses she had a pretty lonely time of it – weeks on end with the rains pouring down and no one of her own kind for company.

At one period the girls' boarding school at Itki was requisitioned by the military and the mission had to take in most of its pupils. Malaria was rife at the time and mosquitos always 'came out in full force' soon after the rains began. So the doctor divided the girls into teams who competed with each other to kill as many of the dangerous insects as possible. Their corpses 'were counted by our tubercular lads' and the winning team received prizes 'of hairpins, press-studs, buttons or boiled sweets'. Moreover, for each 25000 mosquitos slaughtered, 'all the boarders had meat for tea'. The 'tubercular lads' lived together in a corner of the compound and it was difficult to keep them occupied – other than with mosquito counting. So the doctor got them to help in the building of a new kitchen, which had to be done between the end of the hot weather and the start of the rains. 'Even when the work began we couldn't hurry too much because the previous layer of mud had to dry before the next was added. We won the race because the roof was on before the rains started. If we had lost, the walls would have liquified and collapsed.'

Dr Thomson obviously had a talent for organizing, extemporizing and initiating new projects to alleviate the desperate economic and climatic conditions in which the people lived. Many of them suffered from diseases related to poor diet and hygiene and the doctor ran courses for the local girls and women using flannelographs and instructive games of her own invention. One of these, called the Health Journey Game, a kind of snakes and ladders played with 'dice or tamarind seeds' suggests the sort of problems she and other health workers had to tackle. Players were penalized for such things as binding leaves on open cuts, eating rice without any vegetables, catching itch at school, walking barefoot over muddy fields (and so risking hookworm) and eating fly-blown sweets from the bazaar. They got ahead by having injections for diptheria and tetanus, installing proper latrines in the house, attending prenatal clinics. Realistically, there was more likelihood of penalty than reward on the players' 'health journey'.

'So I used to go out to the village women and teach them the fundamentals of hygiene and diet, knowing that, when I returned a month later, I'd have to begin at the beginning again. And with the patients in hospital, you know they're going back to the same set of circumstances and this particular disease will inevitably recur.' This is from Mrs Eve Ross, a trained nurse who admitted that it was 'not really the missionary drive but the medical drive that sent me to India'. She too had been inspired by reading *Mother India* and wanted to help Indian peasant women. Sometimes she'd ask a woman how old she was, 'And she'd work out that she'd started menstruating so many years ago and therefore must be, say, about thirty – and she looked fifty already. Careworn, used up. As this was my own age at the time, I used to think, "Oh my goodness, life has treated us very very differently indeed."'

Mrs Ross worked for a while with the Dom tribe of outcastes among whom the traditional occupations were thieving for the men and prostitution for the women. 'The simple fact of conversion', she decided, 'doesn't produce any noticeable change at all in the way of life of [the convert].' And it took 'three generations of mission school education' before they started to change their ways . . . But was that the right thing to do anyway, she wondered, and confessed that her own faith in God was 'very shaken during those five years in Akbarpur' – a mission in the United Provinces, without radio or telephone, without any mental stimulus or companionship and where she felt 'soul and spirit starved'.

The most enjoyable part of her work was with the children in the small orphanage attached to the mission compound. The little orphans 'responded so to being loved' and she was particularly protective of the girls who grew to be 'desirable wives because there were no in-laws to butt in and interfere with a husband's wishes'. When a lad arrived at the mission as a potential mate for one of them, she would sit nearby at their first meeting, and the girl – probably no more than eleven or twelve years old – 'would come and whisper to me whether she did or did not want to marry that one'.

The ways of the country were very harsh by Western standards and it was difficult to introduce any religious change of heart among those for whom Christ was just one of many gods. Reluctantly, Mrs Ross came to the conclusion that 'those missionaries who went out with a burning zeal to win the world for Christ, believing they were offering Indians a pearl of great price, met with very little success I'm afraid'. And she felt that, in the end, all her own medical efforts were 'like trying to empty the ocean with a teaspoon'.

Nurse Ross is one of the few missionaries openly to express those feelings of doubt, discouragement and failure that must have afflicted many on occasions. Usually these were kept at bay by the sheer pressure of hard, practical work and, even if the number of true and lasting conversions was small, missionaries saw themselves as Christian examplars, 'trying to show a way of life of caring about other people.'

That view was expressed by Mrs Rosalie Roberts who'd been inspired to her life's work by just that visionary ideal of devoted, selfless service. During her nurse's training she heard a talk given by a mission doctor about his work. 'He gave such a vivid picture of life out there, working in a mud hut, operating on a verandah with only oil lamps so that he couldn't do surgery at night, with all the people crowding around, and the dust and everywhere so unsuitable, but he carried on anyway . . .' And that 'fired me to carry on and finish my traning and it worked out just right.' And so there is a sense of rightness to hear Mrs Roberts saying in a radio interview thirty years later, 'I think that the smell of paraffin takes me back to India more than anything, because for so many years we had nothing but paraffin lamps for lights and even, in one place, we cooked on a paraffin stove and had paraffin heaters . . . [And there were] the jobs of lighting the lamps, cleaning them and, if you went round a village just before sunset, every woman would be in her doorway cleaning her lamps and filling them because that's her last task before dark.'

Rosalie first went out to India in 1926 to work in a mission hospital in West Bengal. After nursing all day she spent her evenings studying Bengali – by the light of an oil lamp that attracted numerous insects including 'great big black beetles with shiny shells that zoomed in with a terrific noise and fell on their backs and made an awful buzzing'. Two years after her arrival a Welsh missionary, Arfon Roberts, arrived at the hospital and he and Rosalie eventually married, he wearing a 'very special Palm Beach suit' for the occasion. They worked together in the mission field for the next ten years, mostly in a hospital on the edge of the jungle – 'Not a high jungle though because the wood was cut every five or six years.'

The mission was a prominent white building on a ridge with an open space of dried mud in front. Skin-and-bone cattle came to graze there and, lacking grass, ate the hospital pillowslips which the dhobies laid out to dry. It was a poor area altogether and the missionaries themselves lived mainly on goats' meat, chickens the size of pigeons and fusty-tasting fish from a static watertank. December and January was the fresh vegetable season – 'a marvellous time'. They sorely missed bread and butter; yeast and a tin of butter came every month by parcel post, but it was poor yeast and the butter was like oil.

While Arfon Roberts was pedalling off on his bicycle for about twenty days of every month, preaching in villages and visiting mission schools, his wife worked in the mission hospital. About two hundred people usually arrived for treatment every day and she soon learned to cope with a series of recurrent problems: patients who purloined the (to them luxurious) red woollen hospital blankets; others who would run back home with stitches left in post-operative wounds that then turned septic; snakes that lived in the drainpipes and had to be dislodged with poles; a water supply that was 'chocolate-coloured' and had to be carefully filtered. She learned too how best to treat the victims of particular seasonal and regional hazards. These included men who got drunk during festivals, goaded buffaloes to fight each other and were then accidentally gored; children who fell into vats of boiling sugar at harvest time; and '. . . poor old grandmas who used to go out to gather leaves to make the leaf-plates which they ate off. That was their job . . . They also made plates to sell and got about a rupee for a thousand. Well perhaps these old ladies would get caught in the jungle by a bear and they'd try to scramble up a tree, but wouldn't be able to get far and the bear would claw right down their backs.'

Wrestling with all this, Mrs Roberts still felt uneasy because their own living standards were high compared to those of the neighbouring Indians. But if they lived too frugally, they became run down and ill themselves – and so less capable of ministering to the people. Buying an orange in the bazaar for her own ailing child, she was aware that its cost would have provided a whole meal for a local family; trying to persuade her patients to eat snails from the ditches as a source of protein, she knew she would baulk at eating them herself. During their last tour of duty, the Roberts lived in Calcutta where conditions were comparatively luxurious. Younger, hungrier missionaries from the jungles used to drop into their city mission sometimes and, remembering her own past experiences, Rosalie gave them 'icecream, nice bread and New Zealand butter which we could get from the cold storage. It was really lovely to be able to give them such treats'. She never solved that

common missionary dilemma of guilt at any self-indul-
gence, the drawbacks of too stringent self-denial, but felt in
the end that their manifestly Christian endeavours had
been worthwhile.

There were a number of female doctors and nurses who
went out to India to take up posts in government service or
in purely secular organizations, who were not, therefore
prey to any kind of 'missionary guilt'. One of the most
highly esteemed organizations was the Lady Minto's
Nursing Association founded in 1904 by the wife of the then
Viceroy as a successor to the Up-Country Nursing Association and with the same aim of 'providing nursing care for
European families'. Its nurses, known as 'Mintos', did not
have to tackle the same extremes of deprivation and
ignorance as those who ministered to the Indian peasantry,
but their work was very challenging for all that and called
for considerable independent resourcefulness. This was
especially true in the earlier days when Minto nurses were
often called to emergency cases in inaccessible regions
where no other European medical aid was available.

'A love of travel and adventure' was, therefore, an
important qualification for the job and Miss Emma
Wilson, one of seven Mintos who sailed out to India from
Tilbury in 1921, certainly possessed it. She'd been a VAD
during the first world war, had been awarded a gold medal
at the end of her later training at Barts and was both
qualified and suited for the life. 'From the minute the
Calcutta Mail pulled out of Victoria Terminus in Bombay
and my first journey in India began, I felt happy', she
wrote. In Calcutta she acquired lengths of white drill for
the making-up of her uniform and was sent off to her first
assignment in Assam.

She and three other Mintos with headquarters in
Shillong were always on call to go to the aid of families in
the farflung planters' communities. There was, for instance, the elderly, recently-widowed planter who went

heavily on the bottle. 'In the various sheds and stores at the tea-gardens under his management he secreted whisky for use during his rounds.' He began to suffer hallucinations and she accompanied him to Calcutta for treatment. During the long train journey he sometimes 'had the delusion that a war was in progress and that the Viceroy was hiding on his roof with stores of arms and ammunition. I exploited this delusion, telling him that on instructions from the illustrious gentleman on the roof, we were to make a getaway. The ruse worked splendidly; he and I exploded with laughter at times and I've never met a more amusing and cheerful DT patient.'

One of the scourges of the region was blackwater fever and a tea-garden doctor who sent her off on one nursing mission made no bones about how serious that could be. '"There's the place, sister," he pointed to a bungalow at the top of one of the nearby hills. "Mrs Sprott's the patient, wife of a miner. She's very ill indeed." He indicated an overhead line of travelling buckets. "You go up in one of those coal buckets. It's the only way to get there." He lowered his voice. "The coffin's been made up. You can sit on it in the bucket. It'll be needed tonight." "Anything to oblige," I said tersely, and determined I'd do my best to see it wasn't . . . The doctor said he'd be up in the morning. After my ride up in the bucket, I deposited the coffin on the verandah, the husband showing no surprise. When I entered the bedroom, I thought I'd never seen anyone looking quite so ill. The patient lay with closed eyes, her dead-white face framed on the pillow by long, loose dark hair.' Sister Wilson nursed Mrs Sprott devotedly and continuously for the the next forty-eight hours. At the end of the second day the patient opened her eyes and announced she liked eggs for her tea. She survived and the empty coffin was sent back downhill in the bucket.

After a period in Assam (where her worst enemy was the car-sickness she always suffered on the winding hill roads) Emma Wilson was posted to the United Provinces for ten years with headquarters at Bareilly. It was 'a typical plains station ... with a small bazaar close to the church, the military hospital, a Club with good grass courts and nearby jungle country with shooting and pig-sticking galore.' In the hottest season she was sent to Naini Tal, a gay social centre with the Boat Club at the end of the lake and dancing at the various hotels every night. 'Hearts were broken and mended again and affairs were numerous, though seldom serious.' There was little time in the Mintos' lives for what Emma termed 'the licking of emotional wounds'. They were frequently on the move, sometimes helping out at one of the Association's own hospitals and clinics, or going to the aid of the military, as when she was rushed to a hospital in the Punjab where enteric fever was rife among the rank and file of a Rifle Brigade. She was billeted in the chaplain's bungalow – a padre was in the bath praying when she arrived – and she was on duty every day for twelve hours at a stretch for three months.

In 1938, after a spell of Home Leave, Miss Wilson was appointed Chief Lady Superintendant of the Minto Association and took up her new administrative responsibilities just before the second world war began. Like many others of her caring kind, she soon found herself having to cope with the pressing priorities and unfamiliar urgencies of wartime ... But that is part of another, later story.

6

A Life of Exemplary Rectitude

'On the whole the idea lingers that European
women were all potential "Mrs Hawksbees"
as so amusingly portrayed by Kipling. Nothing could be further from the truth. We
seemed to lead a life of exemplary rectitude, to
the point of stuffiness by modern standards.
But we were very conscious of the proper
image required of the consorts of the "Men
who Ruled India".'

Mrs K.M. Mullan

Many British women who lived in India during this period
did not do so in their own professional right or because God
called them to labour there, they trod no red carpets, dwelt
in no jungli outposts – they were there simply because it
was where their fathers and/or their husbands worked.
Invariably, they and their menfolk believed in the intrinsic
right of the British to rule India and, as Mrs Mullan
suggests, both sexes usually conformed to the patterns of
social behaviour considered appropriate to their status.

British wives worried about status (which depended
entirely on their husbands' positions), and about the
difficulties of maintaining it on budgets that were sometimes quite limited. They worried about school fees,
doctors' bills, holiday expenses and about the problems
caused by long periods of separation from children and
older relatives. They worried too about their servants –
their wages, their illnesses, their foibles and failings, even
though, as Mrs Mullan says, 'the paternalistic system was
never questioned'. They suffered from homesickness and
loneliness sometimes and some regretted the lack of useful

occupation. These were the commonly felt drawbacks of living in India; the highlights were Christmas camps, going 'on tour', home leaves, hot-weather escapes to the hills.

But that is only an outline of the typical Indian experience, it's the individual accounts that give it substance and diversity. In one regard, however, there is a remarkable degree of unanimity – all those who spent their early childhood there remember it as utterly golden! 'I had such a totally happy childhood in India for the first seven years of my life that nothing could really hurt me too badly afterwards,' said Mrs Maud Kennedy. 'It gave me a tremendous sense of security and comfort that has lasted for the rest of my life and I can always return to the sweet memory of it in time of trouble.'

That sentiment – of happiness enough for a lifetime – is often re-echoed and evoked most strongly by recollections of special childhood celebrations, such as birthdays. Wrote Erica Farquarson, 'Our birthdays were pure joy . . . One woke in the morning with a glorious feeling of anticipation and, after the usual walk, came the breathless moment of entering . . . the dining-room surrounded by the family, butler and ayah salaaming and a sort of excited bustle from the passage leading to the servants' quarters where the rest of the staff were peering round the door . . . There, drawn up to the table was the prettiest sight – a throne fit for a princess. An ordinary everyday chair was transformed. A canopy covered it, made of paper frills and flowers and the whole chair was covered in this way in blues, pinks, greens and yellows. You were almost afraid to touch it. This was your seat of honour for your special day. There you sat, lost in wonder, gifts were given and the merry breakfast went on around you. But for a small girl in her fairy-like throne lost in joy and wonder, it was the essence of beauty, fragile, not to be clutched or grasped . . . an eversweet vision of all that life could be . . . The memory catches at the throat still. A rainbow of joy.'

On her seventh birthday, Dorothy Middleton had a note from her father to 'go into the garden and see –'. And there she saw, as she still can in her mind's eye, 'a gravel sweep, rose bushes galore, a cloud of butterflies; beyond the green lawn and on its grass two little white tents just big enough for a seven-year-old child to enter without stooping. One was a *shuldari*, the ordinary camp tent . . . the other a more elaborate "Swiss Cottage" with an awning over the entry. One was for me, one for my brother – such wonderful things for two children.' Their pet hens also added to the fun of these tents. They had two at first, 'a cock and a hen called Adam and Eve, joined later by a hen called Mary. She was a stupid bird and when the tents were pitched in the garden she took to laying an egg daily on a tent roof. Being rather a stout bird, her body made a nice cosy depression and when she got up with a proud cackle, the tent tightened again and the egg fell with a crash to the ground and she was left clucking in a puzzled way with no egg. My father laughed and laughed at this, but we could never persuade her into a proper nest as long as there was a tent to lay an egg on!'

Pets were very much a part of childhood: no dogs usually for fear of rabies, and little mention of cats, but instead those hens, pigeons, parakeets, deer, sheep, goats and, of course, ponies. Monica Francis Clough had an adored pony called Ginger that she used to ride around her 'little kingdom' of the Finlay & Co's tea estate along the High Ridge in Trevancore. Monica was born there in 1922 and knew little of the wide world beyond the High Ridge in which she felt totally – and happily – 'encapsulated'.

But Monica's mother, Marjorie, whose experiences she also sketches in her memoir, did not fit in so easily. She'd arrived in South India in 1920, the young, inexperienced bride of a planter, Eric Francis. Their first home (to which Eric took her from the railhead on the pillion of his motor-cycle) had a leaky thatched roof where rats, rat-snakes and mongooses 'played endless lethal chases'. It was equipped

Olivia Hamilton and her husband and dog crossing a river on inflated animal skins.

Olivia Hamilton and her husband with the morning's bag – 58 partridges and four hares.

Sketches by Kate Farran of the Races at Annandale, a journey by rickshaw and a Ladies' Shooting Competition (army wives were often keen competitors).

On the Road
to
Mashobra

Shooting Competition
Tuesday April 22nd

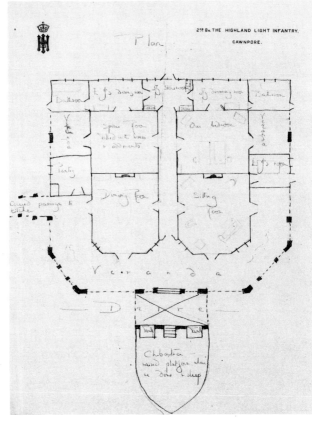

Opposite page
Top Florence Meiklejohn on tour.
Bottom Sketch of a typical army officer's cantonment bungalow.

Dr Claire Thomson.

One of Dr Thomson's 'health games'; tamarind seeds were used as counters.

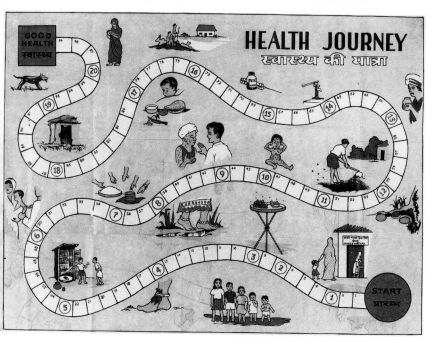

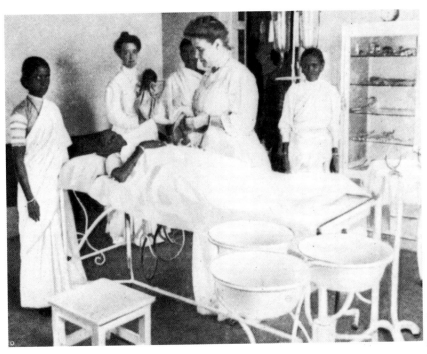

Dr Ida Scudder on her ward rounds.

Dr Scudder on her rural rounds in her first Peugeot.

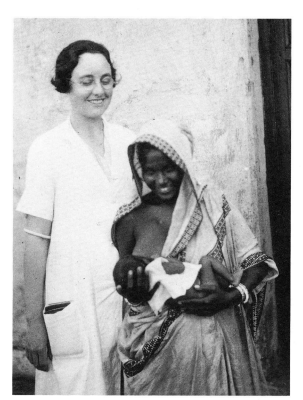

right Dr Honor Wilkins
with a patient.
below left Honor Wilkins
with her baby son, David.
below right Dr Honor
Wilkins and family.

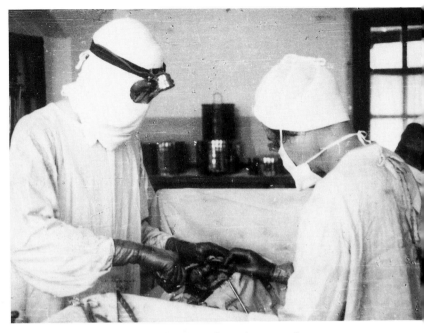

The doctors Wilkins performing a Caesarian operation.

The Clay family on tour; their progress comparable to 'the children of Israel on the march'.

with bathrooms, washstands, enamelled commodes, 'incredibly lumpy beds and battered blackwood chairs'. But Eric 'had promised her a palace'. When Marjorie's trousseau trunks from Home eventually arrived, they'd been driven through flooded rivers on bullock carts and most of their contents were ruined.

It was not a good beginning and, as her daughter later realized, Marjorie often felt anxious and insecure about the country. She expressed these feelings in, for instance, a positive obsession with hygiene. '"Don't touch that, dear, it's from the bazaar", was a frequent admonition, and even the annas had to be washed before putting in the church collection box because, "You don't know where they've been".' Marjorie didn't 'frat' with Indians or learn Tamil or take up riding and, when Monica was a baby, found herself very much alone.

Her nearest British neighbours lived six miles away and Eric was off to take the muster for his labour force early every morning. The labourers were summoned by the blowing of a large conch shell, 'its melancholy, penetrating booming noise . . . signalling the start of the day's work and its close about five o'clock'. Sometimes, in the afternoons, ladies came to call on Mrs Francis, 'with all the formality of the age. Gaunt, sunburnt ladies getting down from their side-saddles. While the syce led the horse away, the lady adjusted her large felt hat and veil, put on a pair of kid gloves and took out her calling cards . . .'

But Mother didn't make friends easily and generally 'kept the country at bay', though her husband was happily at home there and so was her daughter. When Monica was about three they settled in an estate bungalow at Sevenmallay, which she grew to love. New furniture was made for it using blackwood felled in the nearby forests and to designs copied from Heal's catalogue. A baby brother came along and 'received court like royalty' when pushed in his pram to his father's factory. To help with the growing household, two formerly outcaste,

Roman Catholic servants from Madurai, called Mary and Anthony were hired.

Mary, the ayah who pushed the pram and called, '"Oh darlin' topee, topee"' whenever Monica ran outdoors, was 'short, plump, smiling, immaculate in white muslin'. She used to run flatfooted alongside that pony Ginger as Monica rode round the estate and, when she lifted the child off, 'she smelt lovely – of coconut-oil and rice-starch, woodsmoke and curry'. Anthony used to tease the children by pulling grotesque faces, '. . . curling his tongue, which was always bright red with betel, and he could look like a temple-carving or one of the bits of the Elephant Table'. The oval blackwood table had been a wedding present from a planter friend; its legs were carved elephant heads with ears as brackets, its top so elaborately carved with flowers and foliage that nothing could stand on it. Mother didn't like it, but it stood in the place of honour in the sitting-room window, dust always gathered in its grooves.

Once a fortnight a 'very lordly dhobi' arrived with clean washing in a pack on his head, and a tailor made regular visits, sitting on the verandah with his Singer sewing machine 'to make new khaki shorts for Eric and copy rather shapeless cotton dresses for Mother and me'. Occasionally Monica spotted 'a shy little man lurking and carrying an indescribable bundle wrapped in the skin of some animal' and which was a sticky morass of 'honey, beeswax, dead bees and twigs'. He belonged to the tribe that collected wild honey in the jungle, sold it and often got drunk on the proceeds – and, if you saw a menacing cloud of wild bees when out on a walk, you had to stand very still and quiet so they wouldn't land on you.

Honey was everyday fare, as were hens, turkeys and rabbits that Mother bred for the pot. She tried gardening too, but 'porcupines ravaged the root crops, jackals ate the ripe pineapples and langer monkeys stripped off the peas'. In any event, much more exciting feasts came from the huge packing case that arrived from Harrods once a year which contained tins of Walls' sausages, Huntley & Palmer biscuits, sardines, dried apple rings, hops enough to make a year's supply of yeast.

Soon after the conch shell's melancholy note signalled the end of the day's labour and dark began to close over the trees, Eric returned to the bungalow. Each evening, 'He drank a whisky and soda which [a servant] brought in on a tray – cut-glass decanter and soda in a thick glass bottle with marble in its neck which the servant pushed down with a wooden spurtle. Pop! I loved to watch the bubbles rising, especially as the fire was always just lit and shone through them.'

On Thursdays Monica's parents had more to talk about over their drinks as the Home Mails arrived, having taken three weeks from England – and she had a Children's Newspaper to read. Then came the weekend. Sometimes they went to the Club, about five miles away, where the men (and some women) played golf or tennis while other women, like Mother, chatted and knitted. Mother didn't have many friends, but found one in Connie, the Irish sister of one of the estate's bachelor planters. Connie sported '. . . a Queen Mum fringe and earphones which always uncoiled madly. She was vague to the point of legend, but played demon bridge and took to dairying.' She made 'Irish butter' that reached them through the internal mail, 'wrapped in banana leaves in a biscuit tin'. It was very good butter and Connie dressed herself on its proceeds.

Mother worked in the Club library once a week with a few other ladies. They '. . . unwrapped bundles of re-turned books, consulted their lists and sent out another half-dozen. Subscribers each had a yard square of oilcloth with attached tapes and their names on in which the books were parcelled. It kept them dry on the tapal-coolie's head during the journey back.' Monica quite enjoyed helping the library ladies, but it was far greater fun to accompany her father on his rounds.

One year a five-mile stretch of road was contracted to be built through the estate and Monica was allowed to hold the surveyor's staff. 'It had to be held steady and straight for such a long time while Eric squinted through a theolodite. But it was very grown up' and also quite 'eerie and exciting to see a proper road with culverts and retaining walls slicing through country where hardly any people had lived before'. Among the few who did were '. . . black, curly-haired, tiny little men who used to shin up trees into their tree-houses' – which she thought 'madly romantic'.

Another thrill was the occasional late-night excursion with her father to Munnar to collect the wages of the tea-estate labourers. These were sent by post from a bank in Trichy 'in wooden boxes about seven inches square, sewn up in hessian and sealed with dammer seals with Imperial Bank in raised letters'. The boxes were heavy because the money was in small coins – the tea pickers having to work about ten hours a day for twelve annas (about an English shilling). In the old post office Monica remembers 'a smoking lamp with a tin reflector hanging above the chest and throwing leaping shadows, the smell of hessian and sealing wax and the banter of other planters waiting, and being allowed to carry one box to the Chev'. This was their car, with running boards and a spare petrol tin strapped to one side and a canvas roof that folded down on wooden struts along the black leather back seats. She and her father drove back in it through the tropical night, the car's electric lamps cutting a swathe through dark that was also lightened by fireflies sparkling in the tangled undergrowth beside the Munnar River. She comments that they had no thought of a security risk – the two of them alone and 'carrying a month's wages for five hundred people'.

Monica Clough's mother emerges from her memoir as a rather lonely woman somewhat at odds with her environment; Margaret Frater's mother, who was also in Trevancore in the 1920s because her husband was an assistant manager of a rubber estate, wrote her own account of the life. The Fraters also lived in an estate bungalow together with a 'mongoose, ants of all colours and sizes and a lot of toddy cats'. The mongoose kept down the snake population; red and black ants carried off the seeds they planted in the garden; white ants ate through half the new carpet during its first night on the floor; the cats lived on the roof and 'their urine trickled down from the ceiling . . . Being nocturnal animals, they were very difficult to get rid of.' Mosquitos and 'other poisonous creepy-crawlies abounded' and were specially attracted by the oil lamps. But when they retired for the night and put out the lamps, 'the mosquito-nets over the beds kept out any breeze, even with windows and doors open' though not 'the eerie and horrible noises of night birds and various prowling animals all out for food'.

After a few years Mr Frater secured 'a manager's billet' and was put in charge of the back-of-beyond Periyar rubber estate. Their new home stood on high banks overlooking the crocodile-infested Periyar River, but the crocs weren't maneaters, so they went swimming anyway. They also had a dugout boat for cruising up-river, but had to watch out for herds of wild elephants, which were a menace. The animals used to lumber across the river, break down and uproot rubber trees, eat their banana crop and smash down fences. All the estate buildings were surrounded by deep trenches to prevent the elephants knocking them down.

The Fraters lived eighty miles from any sort of entertainment, so they made themselves a golf course and a small croquet lawn and 'invested in a radio which, at that time in India, was quite a novelty. It was a box affair and coils had to be changed by hand to get the different wavelengths . . . Hearing the time from Big Ben, the News and all the latest concerts and plays, we felt we were not now so isolated and alone, for recently we'd been cut off for some weeks by floods.' Mrs Frater was expecting her third child at the time and had to make a horrifying journey to

Ootacumund through those still-rising flood waters. They went by open boat, car, bullock cart, crowded train and in a makeshift trolley in mid air across a rushing torrent where the railway lines had been washed away.

Planters and their families stuck together, talked shop together, ranked themselves in their own hierarchies. It was rather the same among 'the railway people', who, like the planters, enjoyed certain perks, suffered certain inconveniences peculiar to their kind. So only a 'railway child' like Edith Dixon experienced the particular joys of travelling for weeks at a time in the family's railway coach. It was a very long coach that could attach to the end of any train, with one very large compartment for a living/dining room, with a table, upper bunks and chairs; other, following compartments contained a bathroom, servants' sleeping quarters and a kitchen.

As her father was a superintendent, their journeys were always leisurely with long stops at every station for him to make his rounds of inspection. Sometimes on Sundays the coach was pulled into a siding and the family went to the nearest garrison church where 'everyone in the congregation seemed to have a title by which he was known and which defined his job' – for example, MO (Medical Officer). Sometimes they stopped for the night in the open country and her father went off to shoot something more tasty for supper than the everlasting stringy chicken. Edith, tucked in her upper bunk, used to look down on her parents eating at the central table by the light of a hanging oil lamp. The bunks were of shiny brown leather with hard little bolsters that she used to dress up and call her babies, and her much-travelled ayah 'a gentle, rustling bundle of muslin', sang lullabies to her before she slept.

The Dixons' more permanent home was a railway bungalow, much like others of its kind with its coiled cobra stool, ivory and brass ornaments in the living room and Chinese porcelain and brocade 'much valued above the local stuff'. A special feature was that the door outside the main bedroom 'had a letter-box in it for the delivery of urgent railway messages'. These were the pre-first world war days when people 'made their own fun' and the railway crowd specialized in musical evenings – father strummed the guitar, mother gave recitations and played the piano for chorus renderings of 'Daisy, Daisy' and 'You Are My Honeysuckle' . . .

Though Edith Dixon left the country when she was seven – waving that agonized good-bye to her father on the Calcutta docks – she yet felt, 'All my childhood was focused into those years. I ceased to be a child, I think, when I left India.' She never returned; had she done so and run true to form, she'd have become a 'railway wife', as did Mrs Hilda Bourne, whose first proper home was a railway bungalow at Arkonam. Except for a Scottish padre and his wife all the British residents were railway folk: Piggott and Prendergast – Traffic; Giles and Hurt – Loco; and Jim Bourne – engineer.

Mrs Bourne adapted easily to the typical railway memsahib's not very arduous daily round which she details thus: '6 a.m. – *chota hazari*, [little breakfast] of toast, butter and fruit out on the verandah, already dressed for riding. 6.30 a.m. Riding in the countryside or practising jumps in Prendy's compound or shooting in fields for snipe or in the scrub for laid grouse, teal, etc. 8.30 a.m. Breakfast, in dressing-gown (after bath). 9 a.m. Jim to office and I interview Cook and Boy. Give out stores and cloth for servants (duster, polishing-cloth for silver, teacloths, glass cloths), take back dirty ones from day before for the dhobi at end of week. 10.30. Dress and accounts with Boy. Write letters, send and answer invitations, reading, sewing. 12.30. Jim back from office for tiffin – or sometimes alone, or women friends come in. 2 p.m. Jim back to office and lay down till four o'clock. Dress again ready for tea. 5ish. Tennis.' She often played with three of the men, her long skirt 'red up to the knees' by the end with the red court's dirt.

Then it was time for another bath and another change of clothes ready for six o'clock 'when go to a "Whisky and Soda" or give one oneself'. Dinner was about eight o'clock and 'Mr and Mrs Piggott, the seniors of the community, kept up the custom of dressing for dinner every night.' The meal was usually quite elaborate, partly because of the railway 'perk' of getting food supplies sent from Madras carriage free. They went through eight courses – Hors d'oeuvres, iced soup (another bonus was supplies of ice from the mail trains), fish, joint and veg, entrée, pudding, savoury, dessert – with the right wines for each course and topped off with coffee. Bedtime came rather soon after all that.

Life did not get too monotonous because the Bournes had to move house seven times in fifteen years and that proved 'a noisy and exhausting business'. Their household possessions were fitted into packing cases and carried to the nearest station on pony or bullock carts. Hilda made lists of everything – an item that featured on every list being the old-fashioned sofa covered with 'roses and cream material' they'd bought from the hotel in Coonor where she and Jim spent their honeymoon. On arrival everything had to be checked, breakages replaced, new cretonne bought for curtains and chair-covers.

Like Edith Dixon's mother, Hilda often went on 'railway tours' with her husband, in a carriage with five compartments. Sometimes, during the evening halts, a forestry officer would drop into the carriage for a drink and 'tell us of jungle doings'. She especially enjoyed the thrill of riding in the inspection trolleys along the lines, for which she prepared a box of stores, bedding and 'accident gear' that was carried by four 'trolley-coolies'.

Touring railway wives, their horizons bounded by stations and sidings, did not get much close, first-hand experience of the country; wives on tour with ICS officers fared better, though, unlike the bona fide junglis, they usually travelled with quite extensive entourages. Mrs Clay, wife of the District Commissioner of Garhwal, compared their progress to 'the children of Israel on the march'. And indeed, remembers her daughter, Audrey, 'it was a fantastically large procession that moved from camp to camp' when the whole family went on tour.

'Breakfast was eaten by the light of a hurricane lantern and off they set. Dozens of coolies carried all the baggage; chairs and beds stuffed into canvas bags and the tents rolled on the poles, the baskets of hens, the flock of sheep and two cows, their calves carried in a sort of hammock slung on a pole. Calves had to accompany their mothers since it was thought that without them the cow would give no milk. If the calf died, it was often stuffed with straw and stood before the cow while she was being milked.'

By starting so early, the new camp site was reached about midday, the coolies were paid off and returned to their villages while the '"officer commanding" quickly had the tents erected, the bearer saw to the making up of the folding chairs of canvas and leather, with wooden legs; the camp beds had under-blankets of pure sheep skin to help ward off the extreme cold of these winter nights at high altitudes, because sleeping bags had not yet come into use. Meanwhile the *khansamah* was building his cooking range from stones and mud, inserting the four little iron grids he carried with him, and generally produced something hot to eat then and there.

Everyone else in the DC's camp was also busy with such chores as fetching water from the nearest river or spring. Water for drinking had to be boiled and cooled at once and wood was collected for that, and to heat the very minimum for the evening tubs. These were the smallest size zinc tubs so that the contents of a four gallon kerosene oil tin . . . should seem as deep as possible. This bathing business was one of the chilliest events of the day. Taken in a draughty extension of the little Swiss-cottage-type tents, made by enclosing with the canvas the overhanging fly at the back, the only form of heating was a small round brazier, burning very fume-producing charcoal, which, though it looked fairly cheerful, gave out almost no warmth. Everything they took had to be as light as possible, so the boxes containing all their clothes, stores, etc. were strong baskets, each with a shallow tray, as in a trunk, and the whole covered with the pelt of some variety of wild animal which made them sturdier and waterproof.'

Despite all the paraphernalia and organization, the exposure to greater extremes of cold and heat, nearly all the mems. found 'touring' a blessed escape from the monotony of out-station life. Mrs Olive Crofton, whose husband was Assistant Commissioner in the United Provinces during the 1920s, couldn't wait to get away from their 'typical out-station, twenty-eight miles from the nearest railway, with four British bungalows and a tiny Club – if all members were present one could get up a game of tennis in the evening'.

Once settled in their camp, she soon realized it was her duty 'to attend to the local sick who arrived expectantly at the door of my tent'. Fortunately, she'd been a VAD during the first world war and she carried with her 'a modest stock of medicines' to alleviate the most frequent complaints – ophthalmia, stomach upsets and malaria. Sometimes people would follow her from camp to camp and 'worked quite surprising faith cures on themselves' – their faith being more efficacious than her doses of quinine, aspirin and castor oil.

Another of Mrs Crofton's duties was to visit the wives of the local landowners and this could be fairly agonizing when they 'insisted on feeding me by hand as if I was a young thrush. It took some resolution to swallow a sweetmeat or banana that had been held for some time in a hot hand.' She also made a point of visiting local schools, where she was invariably greeted with a vociferous chorus of welcome. Arriving ahead of her husband at one village, she had to face a particularly grand reception committee.

She and her horse were positively lassooed with flower garlands, a band struck up, villagers salaamed on either side and she was guided through a triumphal arch of leaves and tinsel. The band, she noticed, was clad 'in the very old red and blue uniforms of the Oxfordshire and Bucks Regiment . . .' And where on earth did they come from, she wondered?

It was an unexpected glimpse into the past of British India that fascinated Olive Crofton. On the same theme, she records another occasion when, after a tea party she and her husband attended with eighty headmen of the district (much speechifying, swarms of flies on the sugar cakes), the guests began to reminisce. They talked of 'some long dead deputy commissioner and what he'd done in their fathers' or grandfathers' time . . . The names mentioned were never those who came to great honour in the wide world, but I wondered whether it wasn't a greater tribute to be remembered in the districts sixty years after you were dead than to be hung around with decorations in your life-time?'

Lady Crofton, as she became, took great pleasure in tracing the forgotten lives and monuments of earlier British residents; Jean Anderson (who became Lady Anderson) touring with her Settlement Officer in the Punjab at about the same time, loved the natural beauty of the countryside – and the whole comical hugger-mugger of riverine 'touring' on the Indus with four boatloads of people. There was a big boat '. . . for all the staff, the zemindar and his hangers-on with eight ponies in the other boat, our two ponies, the chaprassie on duty, two coolies with tiffin baskets and more staff in the third boat' and, in the smallest, a kind of dinghy, her baby son and his ayah. Tagging along also were 'a couple of saints, *zaildars* of a holy family, one of whom helped me to wind my wool when I needed it'.

The tiffin-in-the-baskets was excellent partridge pie, beer, bread and cheese. After consuming it, her husband 'J' went to inspect the fields while she 'baked, did some accounts, some mending, washed my hair, sat on the boat roof sunning with the dogs who'd also had a hair wash. Now we go duck-shooting from the boat . . .' It was sunset; the most beautiful time: 'Sky and water pink and gold and greeny-blue and, at the sides, where the reflections of the tamarisk trees were, black and mysterious.' They killed their quarry; could scarcely fail to in countryside where so many birds flew – 'darling little blue kingfishers and big marbled ones who hover over the water with querulous squawks and then suddenly dive and carry off fish – cormorants, paddy birds, fish eagles and hundreds of ducks'. It was 'nearly dark when we turned to come home under a darling baby moon whose light glinted along the gun-barrels. Another boat full of hunters passed us as we turned. The men had lit a fire and you can imagine what a picture they made bending over it, with the reflections in the water.'

But travelling with such quantities of people wasn't always such plain sailing. 'Things always go wrong at Alipur', Mrs Anderson wrote crossly to her mother one day, during an overland tour. 'It's a most depressing place . . . Next morning all the servants grumbling and quarrelling among themselves. The bearer had fever. We had new camels and there were awful muddles about loading them. 'J' very worried about work; baby distinctly squealy and the servants went off leaving dogs behind and nothing in which to pack up half a heron (a present from the *munshi*) which was to constitute our dinner . . . Luckily a basket with some Government papers inside was collected from somewhere, the remains of the feast added to them and sent off in the *munshi's* tonga.'

As they rode along the usual 'snowball' effect began '. . . until we had gathered about ten *sowaris* and another local saint – a most repulsive looking old villain in a tonga'. The 'saint' sported 'brilliant yellow boots under his robe and blessed people; but, having been made an Honorary Magistrate' he 'accumulated much wealth by sending people to jail and buying up their possessions'. What annoyed Jean Anderson much more than the rumours of local corruption was what she saw as the niggardliness of the Government's rewards to her husband who worried constantly over such matters. He 'gives his heart and soul to the work', she declared, 'going at it for five months without a pause' – and then they heard their financial allowances might be cut.

Inadequate salaries was a recurring problem especially for young couples. There was the children's education to pay for, the expense of travel within India, and the general keeping up of appearances – not to mention unexpected medical bills or the cost of replacing damaged household goods. Viola Bayley was one of the relatively few to come out in the open and say that, when living on the Frontier, they worried a lot about money. They had to 'weigh up how ill a child was before calling the doctor because of his heavy fees' and it was hard not to envy the better-paid ICS 'with its galaxy of senior posts'. Yet Betsy Macdonald says of her mother (whose husband occupied such a senior post) that, though she always looked one of the best dressed, she had little money to spend and often made clothes herself, 'or draped a sari to a piece of material to look like the latest model'.

Mrs Henderson, the wife of an agriculturist, deplored the fact that, despite one's inclination and the expenses involved, one was forced by custom 'to keep up a certain style' – and pretend to be free from such trivialities as shortage of cash. She and her husband once happened to meet a senior sahib in the Taj Hotel who asked, ' "Mrs Henderson, we never see you in the hills. Why don't you come up to Simla?" I hadn't anything to say. Where were we to get the money? I hadn't the clothes. We had two children at school and that took a great deal of the money we had.' Nor could all who *did* get to hill stations afford to participate in their high life style. Young wives – pregnant, escaping the heat of the plains, convalescing – often stayed together in poky little boarding and guest houses which advertized themselves as being 'very good with children' and were run by former governesses or housekeepers. Or they rented little hill houses furnished with a bare minimum of lumpy beds, bamboo tables, enormous, creaky old wardrobes. They did not have the financial or sartorial wherewithal to attend the grand functions, even if they'd been invited; instead, during the weeks of warm rain, they coped with confined, fidgety children and lots of ever-damp washing.

For many therefore the Christmas holidays were much more enjoyable – when it was the custom to join up with some congenial friends and go off into camp. Mrs M. Walsh captures the spirit of it in a short evocation: 'We shot all day and back in the evening with the sun setting. Tea or whisky with Christmas cakes ordered from the Army & Navy. Dimly-lit bedroom tent with bathroom, daughter over-excited and singing Good King Wenceslas to her. Sherry by the fire and the gramophone lifting spirits and everyone clean and cheerful after warm baths. "Charles" the turkey rich and fat on the plates (eating out of our hands two days ago), crystallized fruits and Bareilly chocolates and toasts to Absent Friends in liqueur brandy and a sad pause with thoughts rushing to Gloucestershire or Yorkshire, London or the New Forest.' Later they went out into cold starlight, dark forest, the scent of wood smoke and dogs barking. 'And Billy climbs into the tin boat and pushes off into the *jhil*. We dance about on the bank and laugh and laugh and at last go off to bed still laughing . . .'

'Billy' and the other hard-working men certainly deserved their jolly Christmas holidays – at least, that is a point made by several of their wives. Mrs Mullan says, 'I was astounded when I went there as a bride because I'd never known the sort of grind that went on every day, files being brought home at night and more files in the morning. The men never seemed to get away from work – always on duty.' The Mullans were in Assam where their 'heaven born' kind were greatly outnumbered by planters and other business people. For them, therefore, life went on 'at two levels. We met socially on every occasion and social life depended on the planters' clubs' – but on the official level things were more formal. On the days when a Deputy Commissioner was inspecting a plantation, for example, he didn't accept the planter's hospitality, 'But even when there were arguments and criticisms the men met in friendly fashion at the Club next day.'

Mrs J. Mills, who first went to India in 1930, was also married to an ICS man working in Assam. They lived in Kohima – a name with later tragic connotations, but at that time an insignificant little place, its small white colony consisting of a bachelor colonel, a major and his wife and some American Baptist missionaries eight miles away, all but the last guarded by troops of the Assam Rifles. Their bungalow was on top of a hill – small, white and on stilts for security against earthquakes. It was the head one in the District and so sported a Union Jack on a flagstaff which was lowered every sunset '. . . with much ceremony and blowing of bugles and stamping of feet and words of command' by the men of the aforesaid Rifles. On Thursdays the whole corps of riflemen Beat the Retreat and her husband took the salute.

For a change of scene Mrs Mills sometimes accompanied her husband on a visit to the Nagas, the tribal people of the surrounding hill country. This could necessitate the crossing of chasms with raging torrents far below – the only 'bridges' being logs of wood with no handrails. When her nerve failed her, she was blindfolded and 'led across by a sure-footed Naga'! On one occasion the Viceroy and his lady visited Kohima and the Nagas came from afar to be presented and performed tribal dances 'in all their finery with beads and hornbill-feather headdresses.' But there wasn't much in the way of entertainment, so Mrs Mills fixed up 'a sort of shed' where planters and their wives came for a weekly Club Night. They rolled back the carpet sometimes and danced to the music of a wind-up gramophone; they played bridge, and tennis on the hard-court in their garden.

Planting families lived in bungalows which 'we tried to make as English as possible', explains Mrs Veronica Westmacott. 'They were very cottagy with thatched roofs. Most of them were built on stilts . . . I had flowered curtains in the sitting room and we had a kind of mock parquet floor made from the best pieces of three-ply sides of tea-chests that had been rejected; laid with dark pieces one way and light the other in diamonds. Well polished, it was most effective.'

The social round outside the home was also as English as could be. There was a season for golf tournaments: 'Will Ladies please supply cakes and sandwiches,' read the notice on the Club Board. Mrs Westmacott, whose husband was one of the leading sportsmen, was expected to oblige and also help with the cricket lunches at which the *pièce de résistance* was inevitably, 'spiced hump'. One had to order a bull's hump (the protuberance used for yokes and harnesses) from the butcher two weeks ahead and it tasted 'delicious pickled in saltpetre and spices, boiled and pressed. It was eaten with Gorgonzola cheese and followed by a trifle with plenty of sherry in it.'

The Ladies' roles in all this were definitely of the handmaiden variety – as Mrs Westmacott noticed. On ordinary Club Nights the planters drove up in their Model T. Fords, some of which 'had collapsed roofs so that, in the rains, a servant sat in the back holding . . . a large umbrella over the sahib's head.' While the men 'talked tea together' at the bar, their wives (who were discouraged from talking shop) were left in the ladies' room just to sit and wait, and send chits by the barmen asking to be taken home. 'No wonder marriages broke up,' she comments feelingly. One recently married planter forgot his wife was waiting and went home without her. 'Everyone thought this very funny, but I thought it was awful.'

Club members sometimes arranged more elaborate entertainments at which, Veronica suggests, the usual standards of 'exemplary rectitude' were, perhaps, somewhat relaxed. 'A very round planter's wife "did" Marie Lloyd; a man played the ukelele – mostly negro spirituals, but often "Ukelele Baby"; another had a concertina but could only play "She was Poor but she was Honest". He used to say that, as the applause was meagre, he'd give us an encore.' They staged 'floorshows' and she did a double act with one of the assistant managers of 'A Bicycle Made for Two' – 'Me in a boater, leg-of-mutton sleeves and a bustle.' Then the ladies from the Assam Oil Field danced in full organdie skirts and sang 'Mary is a Grand Old Name'.

A real spectacular was a night-time show held on the tennis court of their bungalow. The court was of thick matted grass with hibiscus, frangipani and coral trees surrounding it. The planters turned on the headlights of their motorcars to provide illumination and into it pranced Veronica to do an opening can-can. The next number was 'The Pipes of Pan in the Moonlight': draped in swirling chiffon Veronica danced among the headlights until Pan rushed in wearing a leopard skin – but he was overexcited, skidded on the dewy grass and fell in a heap at her feet.

Such occasions were the greatest of fun, as were Planters' Weeks when everyone gathered for race meetings, games and dancing and 'the absolute Heaven' of a week's stay in Shillong – where there were much missed shops, cinemas and hairdressers. New Year was the time of the 'jungle drives' when they took off with picnic baskets on the backs of elephants and the sahibs 'shot whatever came out'. During the cold weather some of them gardened with great enthusiasm, and in due course there followed competitions at the Club to see who came in with the first buttonhole of sweet peas, the first of the season's cauliflowers. When the hottest weather came round again, butter and milk were kept just edible by packing in straw baskets or earthenware jars which were suspended under trees with a boy to pour water over them. Every day the planters' wives – in common with their compatriots elsewhere – supervised the boiling of milk and water to kill off germs, the washing of fruit and vegetables with permanganate of potash, the spraying of the kitchen quarters against the new-born swarms of flies.

Elderly women, who took all this in their stride when they were young wives, look back on it in some amazement. Exclaimed Mrs Mullan; 'I mean when you see the glossy magazines now, you wonder how we managed to exist at all!' But they did; the great majority of them survived – and remember those distant times with pleasurable nostalgia. 'I spent the happiest days of my life there,' said Mrs J. Mills, remembering that small white bungalow on the hill at Kohima.

7

The Colossal Reality

'What worried me most was my ignorance of
the colossal reality of India.'

Mrs Margaret Cousins

Practically all the women who feature in this book so far
viewed the people of India from a considerable distance.
Even if they spoke a native language fluently it was
extremely rare for genuine friendships on an equal basis to
develop between the races. Few British residents made any
serious study of the art and culture of the country and few
were influenced by its spiritual doctrines. Certainly, during
this period, there was no equivalent of the widespread
Western enthusiasm for Eastern religions that developed
later. Neither did the British on the whole (particularly
women) have much sympathy with or understanding of the
Freedom for India Movement. Indian politics generally
'were a sort of irritation that one hoped not to have to take
too seriously,' as one ICS wife put it. In short, few of them
worried much about their ignorance of the country's
'colossal reality'.

But there were some exceptions: people who were
instinctively attracted to Indian ways of thought, who
admired certain Indian values, and who therefore ident-
ified with the political aspirations of Indian leaders. In
consequence, they were bound to question the rightness of
British rule and to find themselves at odds with many of
their compatriots.

Mrs Margaret Cousins was one such exception and
another was Miss Marjorie Sykes. Her father, who greatly
influenced her, had been the headmaster of a village school

in Yorkshire for many years and it was from him she absorbed the idea that children with the fewest opportunities should receive the very best education. She succeeded in getting to Cambridge and, while there, regularly attended 'International Teas' where she was inspired by the radical ideas of political and social reform discussed by students from overseas. Indian students were among the most vociferous and it was they who first aroused her interest in their homeland. A drive to persuade graduates to undertake educational work in the colonies found a willing recruit in Miss Sykes and, in 1928, she accepted a teaching post at the Bentinck High School for Girls in Madras.

It was a fairly unexceptional first step, but Miss Sykes did not follow it up in the conventional way. For instance, she did not, on arrival, go to Government House to sign the Visitors' Book. As Desirée Battye explained, it was from these books that the names were culled of those who would receive invitations to various social and official functions. The great majority of new British arrivals signed up – quickly, eagerly, perhaps dutifully – but Miss Sykes declined to do so. It was a significant decision and an indicator of the way she chose to pursue her unusual and fascinating career in the country for the next fifty years.

The first political event she remembers witnessing soon after her arrival was a black-flag procession through the Madras streets of people shouting 'Go Back Simon'. This was a demonstration against the commission, headed by Sir John Simon, which had been set up to review proposals for self-government, but which did not include a single Indian member. This insulting omission aroused widespread resentment – and Miss Sykes' reaction was an immediate and instinctive sympathy with the protesters.

During the ten years that she worked in Madras, Marjorie Sykes continued to behave in a manner considered quite wayward for a young female teacher of the time.

She 'got ticked off' by her superiors for riding a bicycle round the streets, for travelling on 'ordinary native buses' and, (worse of all) for wearking *khadi*. This was the locally-woven cloth that Mahatma Gandhi urged all his followers to adopt as a protest against the importation of foreign materials and was thus a symbol of her growing affinity with his cause. 'From the very first year I began to wear *khadi* and I have done regularly ever since,' she explained firmly.

During her off-duty hours Miss Sykes became friendly with an Indian leader of the Congress Movement in the South and attended meetings and discussions about the country's future. She once went to stay in his *ashram* and learned to spin – a gentle enough act which was, at that time, a political gesture. It was, she wrote, her 'father's disregard of anything like success' that prepared her to respond so wholeheartedly to Gandhi's ideal of a non-violent, non-competitive way of life. For her, his views represented 'a kind of working out in practice of something I'd already felt to be fundamental'. These early, first-hand experiences of Indian life helped her to understand more clearly 'the possibly destructive effects on other cultures of the impact of a technologically very advanced culture' – an idea she'd first pursued in the abstract as it were, when at Cambridge.

Inevitably, therefore, she became increasingly critical of the British-based educational curriculum and system of values which prevailed in the government-aided schools where she and her colleagues taught. In her opinion, there was an urgent need for 'something more Indian, more independent' and she felt that the existing educational current 'ran in the opposite direction from what I really believed was good for the children'. For her, the conflict was brought to a head in 1937 with the publication of Gandhi's 'epoch-making views on education' which burst upon her as 'a kind of enlightenment'. Soon afterwards she left the employ of the British Government for good and, the

following year, was invited to join the staff of Rabindranath Tagore's community at Santiniketan in Bengal.

Tagore, an elderly man by that time, had gained an
international reputation as a poet, philosopher and educ-
ator, and the Santiniketan community, which he'd founded
in 1922, had 'a very lively atmosphere indeed' when Miss
Sykes joined it. Its founder's magnetic personality had
attracted a number of brilliant teachers and thoughtful
disciples from Europe, America, other parts of Asia, and a
number of original educational and social projects were
going forward.

These included training courses in health and medicine,
a farm for improving crop yields, a craft school for boys
and, for girls, courses in Indian art, music and dancing.
Daughters from highly respectable families were encouraged to perform, which was a great innovation and
represented a complete break from the confines of the
purdah past when the only females to appear on stage were
prostitutes. It was, however, in accordance with Tagore's
belief that the minds and bodies of all human beings should
have the chance to express themselves in harmony. With
this in view, he sought also to rejuvenate the ancient,
rurally-based art forms of the people and hoped, by so
doing, to combat what Miss Sykes termed, the 'city-bred
spirit of progress' which was threatening the country.

Marjorie found the life of the community inspiring,
thought-provoking and congenial to her own spirit, and it
was there that she 'began to think about the deeper
implications of the Nationalist Movement'. She had become a Quaker and was thus particularly responsive to
both Tagore's and Gandhi's emphasis on mutual, peaceful
cooperation instead of independent, competitive self-asser-
tion. The two spiritual leaders were good friends at this
period and she had her first of many meetings with Gandhi
at the end of 1938.

Her work at Santiniketan brought her into close contact
with the realities of Indian rural life and with village

teachers whose humble endeavours to put across the basics of education to their less than privileged pupils again reminded her of her father's example. Having already learned the South Indian languages, she now set herself to master Bengali and had every inducement to succeed because it was the language in which Tagore wrote. 'He liked to compose songs in the first light of dawn,' Miss Sykes explained. 'And he would then send a messenger to the girls' hostel – of which I was in charge – asking for a particular student who had a very good ear for music. She had to sing the words he'd just composed and write the song down.'

During this period, Tagore also wrote a number of short stories which were 'mainly comic skits of sophisticated Calcutta life'. When he'd finished one to his liking, he would 'send an invitation round in one of the children's notebooks he always used for us to attend a reading in his house. He was a pretty good actor and told the stories through both conversation and gesture – it was all very funny, very Bengali.'

After months of concentrated study, Marjorie Sykes was able to understand most of the master's performances and, when he began writing some of his childhood reminiscences, he asked her to translate them into English. Quantities of children's notebooks crammed with his handwriting then began to arrive at her hostel, but before she could start translating, 'he'd send for them back again and fill in the opposite pages. He just kept subtracting and adding to the original all the time which made things rather difficult.' Nevertheless, he must have been pleased with her efforts because he asked her also to retranslate three of his plays. Two, based on Buddhist legends, stressed the rights of women and the third, *Free Stream*, 'showed in mythological form his great concern with growing violence in the world.'

Rabindranath Tagore died in 1941 before he'd finished the final version of his reminiscences and, soon afterwards, Miss Sykes left Santiniketan. Later on she became a

member of Gandhi's *ashram* and was at a Conference in
1944 when he stated his opinions on the teaching of English
in post-Independence schools – a subject she had often
pondered. Later still, she acted as an 'unofficial envoy' to
mediate in long-standing hostilities between the Naga tribe
and the Indians, which led her to endorse Gandhi's view –
that peace and unity are achieved not through the enforce-
ment of uniformity but within 'the variety of the pattern of
differing cultures'. Miss Sykes, now in her nineties, is
saddened that Indian society does not seem to be develop-
ing in the way she hoped, that its 'young people are not
radical enough', and that many of them seem 'geared
towards competition rather than cooperation'. But, as an
Indian citizen, she cannot quite face the idea of leaving the
beloved country 'where I belong' for the last time.

Another woman whose youthful idealism was fired during
the years she spent at Cambridge was Miss Maisie Wright,
who first went to India in the same year as Miss Sykes. It
was while studying at the university that she first heard
about the work of the University Women's Settlement in
Bombay, originally established by a group of Cambridge
women in the 1890s. There were several Settlements in
Britain at the time, based on the ideal of the privileged
sharing their talents with the less fortunate, and Miss
Wright joined the one in London's Docklands before going
out to India as a Settlement social worker.

The organization was based in a large private house in
the Gamdevi district of Bombay and proved to be 'a very
small affair indeed', with only three other British women on
the staff. On first arrival, Miss Wright *did* sign the Visitors'
Book at Government House, but in most other respects the
lives of the Settlement workers seldom impinged on the
social rounds of the foreign community. For instance,
Maisie spent two years in Bombay before she ever rode a
horse and only visited the famous Yacht Club once during
her five-year stay there.

A main aim of the work in India was 'to encourage the more enlightened and adventurous Indian women to take part in public life' and to educate girls towards the same end. This was an uphill task, Maisie discovered, and she was rather discouraged by the many women who declined to help the less fortunate of their sex. A few wealthy Parsee women did a great deal, but others made the excuse that they couldn't leave their homes when menstruating (at which times they had to sit on a special iron chair and refrain from using the telephone) or they were otherwise occupied with family weddings, births, periods of mourning. In an effort to change these attitudes, Miss Wright started a 'social training' class in which she explained the entirely novel concept of 'social work' and tried to create in her students 'a desire to do something for the poorer women in their own city'.

There was, of course, much useful work she could do herself and she began by teaching English and History to a very mixed class of Hindus, Jews, Parsees, Christians and one Moslem. This last pupil she also taught to skip on her flat roof, 'because it was the only form of exercise she ever got'. She helped at the League of Mercy that offered refuge to girls who had escaped from the city's many brothels and, the next year, started a sewing class in the women's block of the jail – where most of the prisoners were prostitutes. She and two Hindu women from her social service group ran the class: 'We take squares of cotton for the women to hem into handkerchiefs. Most of them have never held a needle in their lives, but they seem to enjoy the novelty as they sit in a circle cross-legged on the floor, holding the cloth in their toes. They are childishly pleased when they complete the hemming of a square and are allowed to keep the handkerchief for themselves.' As these scraps of cloth were their sole possessions, they often stole them from each other, which led to 'uproars of accusation'.

Another English woman who tried to help the city's

numerous prostitutes during the same period was Miss
Denise Dane. Her father had been a Governor of the
Pubjab in Lord Curzon's time; she trained as a nurse and
worked for several years at St George's Hospital in
Bombay. Miss Dane felt 'desperately sorry' for most of the
women, who were of various races – black, European,
Eurasian as well as Indian. The fairest could charge up to
ten rupees when they were young, but the rate slipped to
two rupees for the darker-skinned and older women, while
'any coolie' could afford those who had sunk to 'Six Anna
Street'. Miss Dane has never forgotten the sad, shrivelled
little face of one Mrs Alipu 'who saw Six Anna Street
hovering closer as each year passed' and for whom 'there
could be no escape other than death'. Most of the women
who attended the hospital were afflicted with tuberculosis
as well as venereal diseases and, in Miss Dane's opinion,
'the do-gooders actually did considerable harm by getting
the brothels closed' because such measures only increased
the incidence of disease.

Another group of women almost as outcast from society
as prostitutes were widows, and Miss Wright regularly
visited the homes set up for them by local philanthropists.
The inmates, she remarked, 'couldn't overcome their
astonishment that I had no husband, no children and no
jewellery!' At one home, called 'The Abode of the Help-
less Ones' there was an opening in the wall facing the
street into which 'an unwanted baby can be slipped
through into a box with a spring and a bell which the
weight of the baby causes to ring'. Widows who had been
coerced into pregnancy abandoned their babies in this
fashion and the home usually had more than a hundred to
look after.

When they grew older some of these waifs were sent to
orphanages such as the one where Miss Wright started a
weekly playgroup for girls between six and fourteen years
old. She was first introduced to them 'in a decayed mansion
managed by an Anglo-Indian matron, a depressed elderly

spinster. They were sitting in a classroom, under instruction from a beggarly looking Muslim woman who was giving them a lesson on India with a map of the country hanging upside down.' As the girls never went beyond these cheerless boundaries they were delighted with the activities Maisie and her student helpers arranged for them. 'In spite of their secluded lives they are a lively bunch, who enjoy any simple pleasure that comes their way. They celebrate their feast days . . . by painting the palms of their hands with henna in elaborate patterns, and as soon as we get inside the gate we are surrounded by upturned palms which we have to inspect and say which we like best.'

The orphan girls' lot was certainly unenviable, but perhaps preferable to that of the children in the Beggars' Home, an institution run by the local authorities to keep beggars off the streets. There, Maisie and her social work students ran another playgroup for about thirty boys and girls which began 'with a game to test cleanliness and tidiness. Then we divide the children into groups for occupations such as clay-modelling, paper-folding, sewing for the girls and most popular of all, the making of scrap-books. The children never see a picture so they love cutting coloured pictures and advertisements from old magazines. I take delightful little babies and teach them to wash themselves. The first time I had this bright idea I led a particularly grubby little girl by the hand to one of the common taps in the yard. I had hardly begun to scrub her when we were surrounded by a group of wildly gesticulating beggars, and I discovered that I had committed the awful fault of washing an outcaste child at a caste tap. Since they were all beggars I did not think they would be so particular, but it seems that one must observe caste even in a Beggars' Home – what unforeseen difficulties the social worker meets in India!'

The work was indeed difficult, tiring, sometimes discouraging and Maisie enjoyed periodic holidays away from it all. In 1929 she went to stay with Sir Akbar and Lady Hydari in

Hyderabad and visited its famous Mahbubia school – just twenty years after Miss Florence Wyld had opened it. She describes it as a modern institution with about 250 pupils, run on the model of an English girls' public school and staffed by women graduates of Oxbridge. Nevertheless, pupils still arrived in closed cars with screened windows and 'ayahs stand with curtains to shield them from view as they alight'. Maisie's hosts were great supporters of the school and renowned for their pro-Western views; meals in their grand household were served at a large table 'set in western-style', yet the grip of purdah was still upon them. When a man not related to the family called on Sir Akbar, 'I was hastily hustled out of the room with other females of the household . . . and we had to stay in the garden in the dark until he had gone', she reported with understandable resentment.

When not working at the Settlement, Miss Wright sometimes helped in various camps for the YWCA, students and Girl Guides. Quite a number of British women were active in the Guiding movement whose members, both Indian and European, were encouraged to take initiatives, enjoy outdoor pastimes, learn practical skills. They were also encouraged to 'keep themselves neat and tidy, with their shoelaces done up', as one ex-Guider explained. 'You see Indian girls were so undervalued that it gave them a greast boost when they saw us actually taking an interest in their personal development and appearance.'

Mrs Iris Portal, who was head of a Girl Guide division when her husband was stationed in Hyderabad, remembers the girls in her charge 'sleeping in tents, learning to cook, tie knots and so on. They loved to sing and to dance round the camp-fire with their saris flapping and their pigtails flying and it was like nothing in their lives before. They'd never had any fun you see, and it was good for them.'

Junior members were called Bluebirds because Brownies was an obviously inappropriate term for Indian youngsters. Viola Bayley tells a nice story about Lady Baden-Powell who, when she visited the country, was cautioned several times to remember this fact in her speeches. But the matter 'so preyed on her mind' that, when confronted with her first flock of Bluebirds, she began, 'And now you – my little Blackbirds!'

Girl Guides invariably rallied loyally round the symbols of the Union Jack and the King-Emperor, but the YWCA students, Miss Wright noted, began to express considerable anti-British sentiments in their round-the-campfire songs. She herself, like most foreigners in what was labelled her circle of 'do-gooders', was very interested in the Freedom for India Movement and attended meetings of the Nationalist Christian Party whose supporters wanted to prove themselves good Nationalists as well as good Christians.

At one of these, held in a packed hall, 'There were several rather theatrical women speakers ending with one Atia Begum, well known in Bombay for her wild flights of fancy. Dressed in a striking heavily embroidered red garment of her own eccentric design, eyes heavily blacked in khol and with grand gestures, she hardly needed a resonant voice and English educated accent to command attention and rouse her audience. Calling on her hearers to break their ancient bonds, rise against the government, advance their own culture and support Indian industries, she exclaimed, "This terrible thing you bind on your necks – this TIE!" The last word was drowned in shouts as men tore off their ties and flung them into the gangway. The stewards gathered up armfuls of ties, which they deposited on the chairman's table. For some minutes ties fell around us like leaves in autumn, until the chairman announced that any remaining ties would be collected at the end of the meeting.'

Miss Wright's sympathy for the freedom movement was reinforced by her occasional encounters with some of her more typical compatriots. An Englishwoman she once met at a hill station thought herself tremendously adventurous because she'd 'travelled alone for three days and seen only Indians'. When visiting an army cantonment, people asked her how long she had been 'in this infernal country' and didn't she 'hate these damned blacks?' She found such attitudes outrageous and shocking and a great contrast to those held by the people with whom she habitually mixed. Undoubtedly they were not so very unusual, but are not the sort of thing often put on record for posterity.

Another element that distanced the British from the Indians was fear – that deep-rooted fear which echoed back through the years to the dreadful events of the Mutiny, in which some of their forebears had been tragically involved. It was natural enough for women to be afraid when, as occasionally happened, they were caught up in the widespread manifestations of nationalist feeling. There were cases of white women being threatened with violence in the bazaars, or being on trains held up by demonstrators lying across the railway lines. A pupil at Simla's Auckland House School in the 1930s remembers riding along the Mall on horseback with a syce behind, 'And all those bloody Congress people sitting on the roads and everywhere in silence. It was very unnerving to ride right through them – just hundreds of people silent.' One wife found herself living for a while in Patna near a large prison that housed many political prisoners 'who used to yell all night and riot'. When her husband was absent on duty, she wondered, 'What I would do if they broke loose one night . . . It made me very uneasy when they were being brought to the prison past our house. They used to shout and roar out . . . It was a most unpleasant feeling.'

So most British women, protected by their menfolk (who usually kept them in ignorance of the political realities), simply averted their attention from such 'unpleasantnesses'. But even in the upper echelons of the British hierarchy – where, quite often, neither fear nor dislike were present – the degree of familiarity with Indians of similar strata was carefully measured.

When Dorothy Middleton's father was Governor of the Central Provinces she had several opportunities for social contact with educated Indians. She was quite young at the time (1927–32), but 'I wish I had paid more attention to what was going on around me for it was a turning point in India's long march to Independence . . . My father was almost unique in his efforts to bring his Indian Ministers into the Province's government and for much of the time British and Indians worked under him in harmony. The part I was asked to play was to help my mother socially and there were regular dinner parties to which Mr Tambe, Mr Ragavendra Rao, Mr Kedar and others were invited, all at one time or another holding portfolios in the Provincial Government . . . I remember that Mr Tambe and Mr Kedar wore western-style dinner jackets, but Mr Rao always wore the dress approved by Gandhi – the long Indian coat and a loin cloth of Indian-spun white cloth, with a small white cap. Their wives never came.

'Conversation on these formal occasions was never allowed to flag and [I would be] sternly reproved afterwards if silence was seen to overtake my table. The parties were of thirty or forty and we sat at little tables, my father at the head of one, my mother at another, and I among the guests at a third. The weather in the C.P. was hotter than in the north – we had no fireplaces – and the mosquitos were a pest. My father invented a device of having large bags like pillowcases for the ladies to pull on over their legs after they sat down. Visitors from England used to start in dismay when the ladies rose and folds of white material slid to the ground apparently from under their skirts.'

Mrs Middleton goes on to point out that 'The formality of such occasions underlines one of the great criticisms of the British in India – that we did not mix on equal terms with local people. Nor, frankly, did we. The dinner parties I've described were extremely formal; Indians were only allowed in our Club as guests, and they rarely, if ever, entertained us. No Indian was ever asked to a dance. The old-fashioned idea was that they wouldn't want to come – and indeed to the wellbred Indian of those days European dancing was unthinkable.'

Indian men of this type would certainly have felt ill at ease attempting a foxtrot and were usually just as status-conscious and touchy about protocol as their British male counterparts. But the womenfolk of the two races some-times contrived to get together on a more relaxed and equal footing, especially when they had a common purpose. Mrs P. Lacey, the wife of an ICS officer, was very active in the National Council of Women in Bihar and Orissa during the 1930s. The organization's aims were to improve girls' educational opportunities, health and welfare care for women and to obtain legal redress for deserted wives whose errant husbands had kept their dowries. It also wanted to 'widen the horizons of women kept within the confines of strict purdah'.

The Council was middle-of-the-road in outlook and the typical British women to join were wives of the ICS, particularly of the educational services. Often possessing professional qualifications, they quickly tired of what Mrs Lacey termed, 'the deadly provincial suburban crowd' one met at the Club. She and her fellow workers arranged purdah meetings to encourage Indian women to talk freely with others outside their own family circles and to think about wider public issues in general. Barriers of distrust and shyness between Indian women were certainly breached and real friendships did develop between the races. Nevertheless, the concept of actually joining together for any community or cooperative purpose (that would cross divisions of caste and custom) did not really progress very far until the outbreak of the second world war.

Some Council members concentrated on improving health care in their particular localities; they encouraged Indian women to train as midwives and health visitors and set up health centres offering nutritional advice and dietary supplements such as vitamin pills and milk. Mrs Lacey was especially keen to improve the standards of primary education in her province so that 'the next generation would be literate'. She visited the ordinary schools in the bazaars and won the confidence of the teachers; she noted down the lack of books, slates, crayons etc and then 'positively pestered' the local authorities concerned to grant more funds for essential supplies.

The Council's endeavours met with some success, but, by the later 1930s, Indian women who were active in the Congress movement began urging their compatriots to dissociate themselves from it because it was part of the British establishment and its leaders were all white. Such women, whom Mrs Lacey called 'revolutionary types', started the All India Women's League instead and some were 'very anti-British'. Others, however, remained on personally friendly terms with their colonial rulers. Remembered one memsahib, 'Our Indian friends were tirelessly making anti-British speeches and joining demonstrations, but they often came to tea and were quite charming.' And Mrs Sarojini Naidu, perhaps the best known of them all, habitually borrowed books from her British friends to read during the next stint in prison to which the British authorities had sentenced her!

An extremely interesting woman who worked closely with Mrs Naidu and spent many highly energetic years campaigning for causes similar to those espoused by the Council was Mrs Margaret Cousins. She was far more radical in her thinking than the average Council member, however, and as an ardent Irishwoman did not identify herself with the ruling British establishment. As a young woman living in Belfast she had been an active member of the Irish Women's Franchise League and later, when living in England, had been sent to Holloway Prison with other celebrated suffragettes. Then, during the first world war,

Margaret and her husband James set sail for India as members of the Theosophical Society. The Society's president and charismatic leader was Mrs Annie Besant, author, social reformer and staunch advocate of the Indian nationalist movement.

The Cousins, who were devoted admirers of Mrs Besant, went to stay at the Society's headquarters in Adyar, near Madras. James, who was of a somewhat meditative temperament, wrote theosophical works, plays and poetry while his wife flung herself into a positive vortex of activities. These brought her into close and constant association with the people of the country at various social levels and soon helped to dispel some of her ignorance of 'India's colossal reality'. Naturally, considering her earlier affiliations, she immediately allied herself with 'that great company of Indian women who were awaiting the signal for emancipation'. The name of the first organization formed to promote that cause was (in its literal English translation), 'The Weaker Sex Improvement Society'. Margaret was one of those who briskly vetoed that, but from it developed the first branch of the Indian Women's Association, with herself as Honorary Secretary.

The movement for women's suffrage in India thus began in 1917 and, as she points out, it was fairly remarkable that Indian women were exercizing political franchise on the same terms as their menfolk within the next decade and before British women had won complete equality at home. In 1919, Mrs Cousins was on the first deputation pressing for the rights of Indian women which appeared before the Montagu-Chelmsford Commission, with Mrs Sarojini Naidu as its chief spokeswoman. It was Margaret's first encounter with the then Viceroy, Lord Chelmsford, 'who struck me as a perfect gentleman but not impressive in intellectual quality'.

One of the deputation's main aims was the improvement of educational opportunities for Indian girls and Mrs Cousins began speaking at public meetings and schools to gain support for that cause. As her experience widened, she became increasingly incensed by the numbers of promising female students whose prospects were blighted by enforced early marriages. She argued that such unions should be made illegal and wrote, 'There grew within me a determination to do all I could to forward all circumstances calculated to bring women into public and legislative life, so that this end and others might be rectified.'

In the course of the next few years she embarked on five 'suffrage campaigns' in which she toured the country extensively, visiting and forming new branches of the Indian Women's Association, addressing gatherings of college students and Girl Guides, coaching women's groups in the mysteries of their voting rights. She and her like-minded colleagues also worked among the poorer classes. They set up residential 'Homes of Service' in urban areas where destitute women could find food and shelter and 'Baby Welcomes' to which babies were brought for regular baths, medical checks – and a sweet to sugar the pill.

Margaret Cousins must have been one of those over whom others marvelled as to how she ever managed to do it all. For, running concurrently with her efforts to bring about political and social reform, she took an active part in schemes for a wider appreciation of Indian arts and philosophy. When the 'New University' was opened at the Theosophical headquarters at Adyar, she was appointed Dean of the Faculty of Fine Arts and began a concentrated study of Indian musical forms. Music, she claimed, was 'an international pathway to world-harmony' and Eastern and Western forms of it should be recognized as essentially complementary.

Another of her enthusiasms was for modern Indian literature and, in her earlier years, she had written the preface to an edition of Rabindranath Tagore's famous work *Gitanjali*. He therefore agreed to meet her soon after her first arrival and she describes him at that time as 'mysteriously refined and gentle, in a fawn cloak from neck to feet . . . His patriarchal beard adding yet unlived years to his toll of little over fifty.' Several years later, she and 'Jim' (whose efforts were mainly directed towards creating new syntheses between Eastern and Western cultures generally) went to stay at Tagore's Santiniketan community. Highlights of their visit were the 'roof-talks' when staff and guests gathered together on the flat roof at dusk to take part in 'free-ranging discussions' on various philosophical, artistic and religious themes. The experience stimulated and uplifted her spirit and 'when, in the starlit silence, the exalted communion ended and the rapt group quietly retired, it was some kind of pain to fall back into actuality'.

But the pull of actuality and the urge to change certain aspects of it were strong within her and she always returned to the challenge of public affairs. In 1923 she became the first woman ever appointed as an Honorary Bench Magistrate and was garlanded with roses and marigolds by Indians in the court when she first took her seat. To her delight, numbers of Indian women voted for the first time in the local elections held later that year and many were also joining the All-India Women's Association and attending its annual conferences.

Mrs Cousins was always there, wearing the outfit worn by all women members of Annie Besant's 'Brotherhood of Service': plain white jacket and skirt, with a blue rope-belt and 'a silver sun-symbol' round her neck. Busily she helped to work out resolutions and organize meetings; she made speeches and encouraged young Indian women to come forward and speak for themselves. In 1928 she persuaded the well-known and powerful Begum of Bhopal to be the Conference President. It was a great success and its conclusion was, she wrote, 'A sight for the Goddesses and any Gods who cared to look on, to see the two venerable old ladies, the Begum and Mrs Annie Besant, full of years of experience and fun, walking hand in hand down the passage to the exit between hundreds of charming, intelligent, free-minded Indian girls and women who saluted them, some in the Hindu way of palm to palm, some in the Mohammedan way of palm to forehead.'

At the following farewell tea, Margaret managed to buttonhole (one imagines she was good at that) Her Excellency, Lady Irwin and outlined to her the scope of the Association's work and its principal aim of 'bringing together women of every religion and political opinion in a sisterhood of cultural and social service'. Her Excellency, she wrote, graciously expressed her pleasure at the all-inclusiveness and political neutrality of this. But such a stance couldn't continue for long as Indian women became more politically aware and allied themselves openly with the freedom movement. So, of course did Margaret and Jim Cousins and Mrs Besant, whom the Government considered something of a nuisance. This was clear sometime later when Mrs Cousins was at a dinner attended by the next Viceroy, Lord Willingdon – who probably regarded her as a colourful eccentric. She crossed swords with his redoubtable wife who 'felt that women's influence was sufficient backstairs'. And she defended the work of Mrs Besant whom the Viceroy referred to as 'that terrible old lady who has given me infinite trouble'.

During the Willingdons' term of office Margaret Cousins became increasingly active, even combative on the political scene. After visiting Gandhi during one of his imprisonments, she felt exceedingly 'exasperated by the meanness of the British authorities'. She attended an enormous public meeting held on the beach at Madras at which Mrs Gandhi was the principal speaker and she herself was a main speaker at the next meeting. She urged her listeners to exercize their right of free speech and her appeal was followed by an Indian 'who declared he would defy the Ordinances. An English police officer ordered the speaker to stop. I broke in and said I endorsed all the man had said. The officer, after some hesitation, arrested me and conducted me to Beach Road between lines of volunteers shouting slogans in my favour.'

She was allowed home after that, but in the eyes of the British authorities, she had gone too far. A notice for her 'preliminary arrest' was served on her two days later and she was brought to trial the next day. In her speech to the Court she announced that during 'seventeen years of living and working with my Indian sisters and brothers . . . I had learned how exploitation and injustice through foreign rule was crushing them down'. The prevailing system of government by ordinance, she announced, was actually 'designed to break the spirit, ruin the health and cripple the resources of all the people in India who are determined to win political freedom'. The press gave that speech a lot of coverage; the judge sentenced her to a year's detention in the women's prison at Vellore; when she arrived there the prison's Governor, Major Khan, gave her quite a welcome and turned out to be 'as nice a jailer as anyone could wish for'.

As she was a political prisoner, Mrs Cousins was allotted a second cell as a sitting room and soon set about making the most of her confinement. She established a routine of early rising, meditation before breakfast and walking a mile after it – which was six times round her enclosure. Then she would 'spin a while and conduct classes in civics, singing and needlework'. By volunteering for 'hard labour', she acquired seedlings to make a little garden and materials for sandboxes for the jail's babies. Sympathizers sent positive 'shoals' of letters, visitors brought fruit and cakes, her ever-loving husband wrote her sonnets.

The year was 1933 and while in prison she received the sad news of Mrs Besant's death, at the age of eighty-six. But one 'so close in spirit . . . seemed always to be just round the corner', and she felt sure she would again be near her in lives to come. Margaret Cousins was freed from prison on 21 October and Jim drove her back to their cottage where she was 'smothered in garlands of flowers. My head was splitting with the noise we had crawled through. My hair was hanging down my shoulders. A procession headed by a country band escorted us on foot from the gate to Krishna Cottage – We were home, and home was heaven.'

Quite unquenched by her experience she resumed all aspects of her work as before. She gave series of lectures on the political awakening of Asian womanhood, on the therapeutic relationship between art and medicine and on 'The World Mother' – a plea for the increase of the female principle in religion and in life generally. She concerned herself with the fate of the Indian 'untouchables' and arranged for talks given by Margaret Sanger on birth control. The seniority of her sixties brought new responsibilities and in 1936 she was President of the 10th All-India Women's Conference which was attended by about 2500 people. At its opening session she was again 'garlanded up to the eyes'; by its close she 'felt still more surely that the future of humanity was with womenhood'.

8

A Mass of Scarlet Cannas

'Kohima was a lovely place set on a spur
jutting out into the valley. It was a well-kept
little station and, as we went to deliver the
mail, one had a glimpse of the Deputy Commissioner's garden where a mass of scarlet
cannas bloomed in the sunshine.'

Lady Olive Crofton, 1943

A viceregal ball was being held in Simla on the September
evening in 1939 when Mrs Viola Bayley heard over the
crackling airwaves news of the invasion of Poland. 'In the
dark of the night, the endless procession of rickshaws
wending their way towards Viceregal Lodge, each with its
own wavering lantern, looked to me wonderfully beautiful
– a trail of glow-worms flitting past the trees as the road
twisted and turned. Everything that night seemed unreal –
a feeling that was to be constantly with us in the months
ahead.'

Some of the real worries began at once, of course: about
children, relatives and friends at Home, about husbands
posted to the European fronts, leaving their wives stran-
ded in India. But such actualities as the bombing of
civilians, blackouts and rationing were remote, almost
unbelievable. Margaret Ussher in Hyderabad remembered hearing news of the latest German victory in
the summer of 1940. 'I went along to the Taskers for tea
and together we sat and listened in to London at 5 p.m.
We were all completely stunned, simply can't believe it's
true. What has happened? Where is it all going to end? . . .
We all feel so upset and so utterly *useless*. If only we could
dig or nurse or do something it would help such a lot.

Instead, we are carrying on as if nothing were happening. However, this last jolt will shake India up a bit . . . I'm going to take First Aid and Nursing courses at the hospital. Begum Sahiba's war contribution can be my time and the use of the car petrol!'

Other British women who, in those early days of the war, felt like Miss Ussher, set about forming committees. The Ladies' General War Committee began in Calcutta in December 1939 and from it subcommittees proliferated to fund-raise for the cause and recruit female volunteers to train in first-aid and welfare work. A messenger service for confidential information was run by women, who were also employed early on as censorship and cipher clerks, for there was a growing need for secrecy and restriction due to the increasing amount of antiwar sentiment in the country.

The Government, determined that the Empire should show a united front to the world in this time of crisis, encouraged a stubborn continuance of the status quo. On the day, in that same dire summer, when news came of the fall of France, the Resident of Kashmir, Sir Denholm Fraser, was due to hold the State's Annual Garden Party. He wired to Delhi for instructions and was told, 'Carry on as normal . . . policy is to show the Indians we are not over perturbed about the war.'

And so, in those beautiful Residency gardens where tall blue delphiniums and pink Kashmir roses were in full bloom, occasional tables were placed under the chenar trees on the lawn just as usual, wrote Desirée Battye. They were spread, as usual, 'with thin, well-peppered cucumber sandwiches, with the cook's special, deliciously moist walnut cake and bowls of strawberries and cream to follow, while servants carried round trays of fragrant china tea and lemon.' The ladies 'were in flowered dresses, with long white gloves and picture hats at an angle, the men in morning-coats'. Indian men wore 'milk-white jodhpurs with apricot-brocaded coats and pugris aglint with gold' and their wives wore flowing, many-coloured saris. Above this peaceful gathering the Union Jack fluttered proudly, as usual, from the Residency flagpole.

That was surely among the last of the imperial scenarios to be apparently quite unruffled by any threat of war. In the ensuing months the news from Europe worsened and people separated from loved ones in danger became increasingly anxious. In an effort to sweeten the lives of the ration-ridden British, one Mrs Margaret Perry set herself up as 'Organizer in India for the Chocolate and Sweets Appeal for Children at Home'. Indian confectioners were pressed into service to manufacture fruit fingers, barley-sugar sticks, bulls-eyes, lollipops and Regal toffees 'made specially hard to suit the English taste'. Posters were circulated with the appeal – 'Please help us to give sweets for this Easter'. Donors were encouraged by the news that, 'over 20,000 lbs of chocolates and sweets had been sent off before Christmas'. The ambrosial cargoes, packed in tin-plate containers and shipped from Calcutta, usually arrived safely at County Hall, London and were distributed to the city's schools and provincial evacuee centres.

In December 1941 the Japanese bombed Pearl Harbour; two months later, Viola Bayley, now working as a cipher clerk, sat typing out decoded messages in her Delhi office: 'I shall never forget the morning when the news came through. While typing one could not watch the tape as it registered the decoded message. Suddenly I realized that the room behind was full of gold braid, and senior officers bent over the tape as it curled out of the machine. There was dead silence except for an occasional 'Good God!' When the message ended there was no need to ask if it was bad news. It was appalling news. The Japanese had seized the water supply. Singapore had surrendered with over 150,000 casualties, and prisoners taken not far short of that number.'

War was no longer a distant, half-unreal threat; it was here, in Asia. Within the incredibly short time of one month Rangoon too had fallen to the Japanese and India was the next, highly vulnerable frontier for the enemy armies to penetrate. As Monica Clough put it, 'Before that we'd all been listening to the European news and often dissolving in floods of tears. Now we had to face round and see that the war was coming from the East.' It made the British in India realize, rather belatedly, that they were not infallible after all, she adds, and their sense of security in the imperial order of things was shattered forever.

Mrs Clough, recently married to a RAF officer, was living in Calcutta at the time, the city most directly affected by the news as refugees from Hong Kong, Singapore and then Rangoon began pouring into it. The earlier arrivals had managed to escape with their wardrobes intact and were recognized in the Clubs by the up-to-date style and quality of their clothes. Soon, Allied troops and men from the retreating Fourteenth Army began to arrive too and Mrs Clough, like many other Calcutta wives, joined the WVS. The organization started in India in 1940 and from then on its members in many parts of the country were actively engaged in raising funds for the war effort.

They made and sold ginger wine, lemon squash, cakes and sweets; they arranged tea dances, tennis, bridge and ping-pong tournaments, dog shows, gymkhanas, baby shows, flag days and sales of work. And – a specially Indian touch – they held purdah parties where Hindu and Moslem ladies received instruction in First Aid and Home Nursing. While older WVS ladies staffed the troop canteens on the Calcutta racecourse, the younger ones were always in demand for dances. 'Cohorts and platoons of us went together', relying on the safety of numbers, Monica Clough reports. For them, dancing was usually more duty than pleasure because they were so outnumbered. Soldiers were issued at the door with a red or a blue ticket and every dance was one colour only so that only half the men at a time could invade the floor – but the ladies were expected to whirl through every dance until they were quite exhausted.

The comparative light-heartedness of those days was short-lived as growing numbers of refugees reached the country. They came by plane, boat, train and on foot, were no longer in the least well-dressed and were suffering from exhaustion, disease, wounds and/or mental instability after their various ordeals. In her book, *Bengal Journey*, Rumer Godden records the work of the Red Cross and St John nurses who met trainloads of evacuees from Burma. Patients lay in rows on the platforms, some with gangrene, others with roughly-amputated limbs and 'after meeting trains all night, lying down in the waiting-room between trains, we could rush home for a change of clothes as we were soaked in sweat and blood' – then return for the day shift.

Ambulance sisters armed with First Aid kits and basic foods were among the first to board the ships from Burma in which refugees had been tightly herded together for the voyage. 'To go down among them was like facing an inferno of panic and pain and fear and noise and smell.' Some vessels had as many as 1800 evacuees aboard, and a few had invariably died on route. Women's organizations set up an Evacuee Bureau to deal with the multifold problems of mothers and children who had lost everything when they fled.

Another organization was for 'Wartime Hospital Supplies' which was divided into sections. In the Receiving and Vetting department, women sat at long counters examining each item sent in by working parties throughout Bengal. The items were then sorted into roller or sewn bandages, gauze dressings, hospital linen or apparel. Indian tailors worked in the Cutting and Preparing department making special items such as loose drawers for burn cases. Other departments dealt with Folding and Tieing, and Packing for dispatch to the battle areas or to hospital ships when they came into port. Red Cross volunteers also sent supplies to able-bodied fighting men: kits containing razor blades, soap, ready-stamped letters, scissors, torches; games of cards and draughts or mouth organs to keep up their spirits, with special condiments for the Indians and combs for the Sikhs.

The Women's Auxiliary Corps of India, modelled roughly on the lines of the ATS was formed in May 1942. Its recruits (called WACIs) were British, Indian, Anglo-Indian and a few Gurkhas – whose menfolk were of well-proven military prowess. Most of the Indian women wore saris, with military-style, khaki jackets over the top – which did look a little odd. By that autumn, about a thousand auxiliaries between the ages of eighteen and fifty had enrolled and were taking over tasks to release men for active service. This was a matter of increasing urgency for the threat of large-scale invasion by the Japanese of the vulnerable regions of Assam and Bengal was very real and the British civilian population were now well aware of it.

Mrs Betty Diamond was the wife of a bank manager living in Bareilly, where, up to 1939, everything was very similar to Ajmeer, where she'd spent her childhood twenty years before and where you still had to 'make your mark in The Book'. But in 1942, orders came to dig slit trenches round all the main town buildings, 'which was quite awful because, I mean, if the Japs had got that far what use was a slit trench going to be? And they simply filled with water and made lovely hideyholes for snakes and scorpions and mosquitos. And it really was rather daft!' But the trenches were duly dug and she dutifully took first aid courses and learned, as per instructions from the military, 'to prepare a room against gas' and stock a go-down on the verandah 'with dry goods for the servants and blankets and candles'.

Another invariable accompaniment of war – rationing – also began to affect the civilian population, and books such as *Fifty Ways to Cook a Chicken* and *Pot Luck* sold well. The latter was a 'Collection of Favourite Recipes from the Ladies of the Bengal Coalfields' and proceeds from its sale were donated to War Funds. It included solid wartime favourites such as Heinz Spaghetti Savoury (tinned spag., sausages, breadcrumbs and onion) and, in the best tradition of Indian housekeeping, hints on the renovation of patent dancing shoes and the curing of prickly heat.

Bengal was rather in the front line, but even in the comparative security of the south, 'Rumours circulated that the Japs were about to invade India and the war felt very near to us', wrote Mrs Frater, the estate manager's wife. 'Sugar, rice, flour, bread and petrol were all rationed. The last was a very serious blow to us, as we were fifty miles away from the doctor and shops.'

In Lahore and Quetta, at the other extremity of the subcontinent, 'even the *burra-mems* sailed about on bikes to save petrol'. Scrap depots were opened there for the collection of bottle tops, newspapers and tins to sell to dealers for the War Fund, (while the ladies of Simla, rather typically, organized 'midnight cabarets' in the same cause). Quetta in wartime had a greatly increased British population – of WACIs, of planters learning military tactics at the Staff College, of nursing sisters 'in white headdresses and red shoulder capes' and of so-called 'abandoned wives' whose husbands had been posted overseas to fight.

One of them, Desirée Battye, who'd married her husband, Stuart, while working in Kashmir, describes the city's lifestyle as pretty frenetic. Its atmosphere, she explains, had long been notorious for having 'a stimulating effect of a sexual kind'. And, in more peaceful times, couples from malarial areas who'd been too long under the sterilizing influence of quinine came there to conceive – and invariably did. A happy result also put down to the 'Quetta water'. Wartime Quetta carried on the tradition apparently, but for recently married 'abandoned' wives like Desirée it was not much fun and her most vivid memory is parting from her husband, who was going off to train for desert warfare. 'I lay in bed in Queen's Road watching Stuart put on his starched khaki uniform with the bush-jacket sleeves rolled up, tie up his boot laces in his exact manner, place his swagger stick under his arm, press his topee firmly on his head – red and navy-blue flash on one side, silver badge of the Prince of Wales three feathers shining in front. It was still dark outside, the porch light shone on the station wagon with an orderly standing stiffly beside the open door. The car-door slammed, tyres rasped on the drive and he was gone. I buried my head in the pillow and sobbed . . .'

As the sorrows, anxieties and deprivations of the formerly distant war came closer, so the work of the women's organizations expanded and they became more directly involved. Their headquarters were usually in Delhi where, by 1943, fears of enemy invasion were particularly rife. Slit trenches had been dug and worried mothers made desperate plans 'to stain their children's faces with walnut juice and send them to native villages with the servants for safety' – a real throwback to the Mutiny days. Though the city was often decorated with signs reading 'British Go Home', it was, in fact, desperately overcrowded with Allied military and civilian personnel.

Every hotel and large house was packed with them, while others stayed in huts and tents in the grounds or on commandeered open spaces. Mrs Margery Hall fetched up there for a while when her husband was recalled to the army. They were billeted in four tents '. . . each the size of a large room and with a brick fireplace, carpeted with dhurries and smelling of canvas and crushed grass'. Their tents were part of a great camp with roads running through large enough for cars and with enough people to create a hive of gossip. There was, for example, the story about the wives of 'two brigadiers called Juicy Lucy and Bloody Mary who surreptitiously changed tents while their husbands did not'.

Lord Wavell had now taken over as Viceroy from Lord Linlithgow, and his lady ran a parcel packing depot in Viceregal Lodge for dispatch to needy families at home. Mrs Gladys Straus, who had played among the city's foundations as a child, was now a 'WACI officer with three pips' working in Wavell's headquarters. 'He was a great lover of poetry and one of my jobs was to type out copies of his favourites. I thought he was a wonderful man really!' Lady Wavell, to whom even officers in khaki skirts still curtsied, used to arrange little suppers for the troops at which each 'was served with a microscopic portion of ham'.

Miss Emma Wilson, Minto nurse now promoted to Chief Lady Superintendent, also had her headquarters in Delhi and her Association now staffed four hospitals and four nursing homes for Europeans and Indians. Good 'Mintos' were hard to find with so many other nursing services on the scene and young nurses were not so easily 'restrained in off-duty hours' in a city full of men in uniform looking for a good time. Her office phone rang 'incessantly' with pleas for medical help – some from those affected by the war, others from sick people no longer able to go Home for cure. Although her cramped office was always noisy and busy, Miss Wilson was fortunately billeted in a family house along Akbar Road that had a beautiful garden – in which she usually slept. How 'I enjoyed those long still nights in the garden with the scent from the flowers – nicotine, stocks, flowering frangipani – perfuming the air. On moonlight nights the garden seemed almost as light as day. The details of the trees were clear, the moon-drenched white flowers appeared dazzling, colours appeared washed out of the other flowers so that all alike seemed white . . . During the hot weather a peacock settled on a tree near my charpoy, his long tail reaching almost to the ground. And how enjoyable to wake in the early morning to the singing birds, the flowering trees . . .'

After breakfasting on the verandah, Emma Wilson usually cycled to her office, for at that time there were few vehicles in Delhi except tongas, whose drivers were 'a nuisance because they never seemed able to decide in time which road to take. And I often found myself entangled with the tonga pony.' She was a well-known figure on the scene and when she cycled to the Club for tennis, her

Lady on an inspection trolley of the kind used by railway engineers.

Veronica Westmacott in her garden with pets.

The sitting-room of a typical planters' bungalow.

Maisie Wright.

University Settlement Women Students' Hostel, Bombay.

A 'purdah picnic' in the hills.

Margaret Cousins and her husband.

Opposite page
Top Margaret Cousins as the first woman magistrate appointed in India in 1923.

Bottom Margaret Cousins actively involved in the Indian political scene.

Margaret Ussher (centre) who left teaching and went to war.

Lady Linlithgow inspecting a WACI parade in Delhi.

The WVS prepare a welcome for
returning troops.

Right and below American soldiers in
Karachi – sketches by April
Swayne-Thomas.

Serving the troops.

Checking the stores.

beloved retriever Solomon trotted behind carrying her racquet. When invited to dine with the Viceroy, she '. . . tossed one end of my lovely long frock over an arm, arranging what was left of the skirt to cover my ankles in a respectable manner, mounted my cycle and happily sped on my way from York Place along Queensway . . . up the Ramp and into the courtyard of the Viceroy's house. The *chaprassis* awaiting the arrival of guests looked horrified at first then, recognizing the unusual form of transport, broke into broad grins and rushed to my assistance as I tried to dismount with decorum.'

Part of Miss Wilson's war work (for which she was awarded a Kaisar-i-Hind gold medal) was serving on committees for the more efficient 'organization of women-power' throughout the country. By this time, female volun-teers (the majority in the WVS) were distributing supplies and running diet kitchens in hospitals, organizing air-raid drills, driving ambulances, helping in clubs for the able-bodied troops and hostels for the convalescents, and setting up more canteens and shops for all military personnel.

A number of these were on station platforms where troop trains passed through on route to the Burma campaign. Rumer Godden describes the Bengal Nagpur European Institute Canteen as a 'long green hut serving hot meals, icecreams for four annas and mammoth sandwiches for three'. It could cater for up to six hundred men in transit, boasted its own band of 'Canteen Cats', held regular dances, concerts, film-shows and housie-housie sessions. Mrs I. James, an army wife, who worked in a similar canteen, remembers being 'taken to the station in an army truck and it was terribly hot and smelly waiting around for the trains to arrive . . . There were Gurkhas, Sikhs, Indians and British aboard usually and each man got a mug of tea, two biscuits and two cigarettes. That much was free to other ranks, but officers could pay if they liked. You had to be very careful not to offer cigarettes to the Sikhs and not to give too many to the Indians – who always pleaded for more.'

Canteens were also set up nearer to the front, into which lorry-loads of men might suddenly come crowding. As Rumer Godden describes the scene: 'Old Mrs M. . . . is serving, Yeena and Meera, Mrs Y.'s schoolgirl children, are buttering buns; the butter runs between the split halves . . . The run is on for iced minerals and, mysteriously in this welter, for bacon. There is a heavy smell of bacon on the air and chocolate from trays of cakes – and of hot old metal from tea-urns. The urns give off a steam of heat, a brassy aura.' Some of the men are 'too hot to speak – dusty filthy necks and arms vivid scarlet, eyes sore from dirt and glare, having been in workshops, airstrips, gun sites under the full sun.' They jostle to the counter, ordering 'Two bacon, one egg, fifty Players, minerals, cuppas, minerals . . .'

Sailors on shore leave from the dangerous coastal waters also needed refreshment. Betsy Macdonald's planter husband joined the Royal Indian Navy and went to sea as commander of a flotilla of 'little ships' trying to oust the Japanese from the Arakan coast. Their base was at Vizagatapam, a port north of Madras, and she moved there by train with 'our belongings, the dogs, a Siamese cat and a hen I'd somehow acquired and who had to travel in the guard's van. The following morning the guard said excitedly, "Memsahib, you have one egg." '

While there she helped to run a WVS canteen for the men of the flotillas, who 'returned to harbour . . . playing their theme tunes over the loudspeakers – "Colonel Bogey" and "Daddy wouldn't buy me a bow wow"'. The canteen was an old building in the bazaar and its kitchen was simply 'an open-air affair with bamboo and chik walls and a rush mat roof, letting in the millions of flies which were a real menace . . . It was a job trying to keep food clean and covered, and water boiled and cooled. This had to be done in large, cleaned kerosene tins on charcoal or wood fires outside, both for drinking and washing up water. The open charcoal fires for cooking in the kitchen often made the heat almost unbearable. At times I would get home and jump into a cold bath and take my sweaty overall off in it; at other times I was lucky and could stop the truck by the sea on my way home and plunge in for a swim.

'Our pani-walla [water-carrier] had to go and draw water from the communal well outside and occasionally would have to return and fetch me to accompany him to keep his rightful place in the queue, as anti-British feelings had spread, even to the shops. As the Indian shopkeepers had, up to now, been so polite, it was upsetting to find some of them would not get to their feet or give one their usual salaam of greeting; they just stared sullenly when I went to purchase . . . food.'

As time went on, 'Imported bacon and butter became scarce and when the Motor-Torpedo-Boats (MTBs) arrived from America, the bacon, butter and other stores which were found packed in the engines were much appreciated. It was a most generous gesture . . . We made many good friends with the MN crews and they went off with little ash-trays or spoons as souvenirs and we used to sit looking at photographs of their families. There was a large American camp near the beach and we felt quite honoured when they asked if they could come and cook their Christmas dinners in our kitchens . . . They had quantities of tinned food supplied to them and generously gave some to us; but they were horrified by our lack of provisions and conveniences.'

'The Yanks' had certainly reached India, bringing with them the usual bundle of mixed blessings for the resident populace. In Karachi, 'They raced through the streets in jeeps, frightened the horses and bullocks and ran over the hens.' In Delhi, people grumbled because they tipped so generously that 'you couldn't get a tonga for love or money'. But the main point about them of course was the vital part they played in keeping the Japanese at bay on the north-east Burmese frontier. It was to Assam therefore that most of the Americans were eventually sent – as Miss

Emma Wilson discovered when she went to inspect her nurses in that troubled region.

At the station she found the train packed full of troops, 'Then a head stuck out of a window and a voice said, "Come in here, ma'am. I'm carrying the U.S. mails and I'm not supposed to let anyone in, but I can't bear to see a dame in a difficulty." I jumped in without delay and dumped my bed-roll on one of the two bunks. My host was a tall Army sergeant who appeared worried, "For goodness sake hide in the bathroom when we're in a station or I'll get into trouble," he said. The sergeant was a famous provider and fed me with American rations, brought large mugs of sweet tea and told me the whole story of his life from birth to the time he joined the army . . . I kept my bargain about hiding in the bathroom . . . and at night we settled ourselves in our respective berths. There were no lights in our compartment. "Good night ma'am." "Good night sergeant." And in two minutes I heard his snores.' In that fashion, after a slow journey of two nights and days, the Lady Superintendent reached Assam.

From the spring of 1942 when Burma fell to the Japanese and soldiers of the retreating Fourteenth Army together with thousands of civilian refugees began pouring across the frontier, Assam had been on a wartime footing. For the British planters and their wives it meant a permanent end to the quiet and relatively easy lives they'd long enjoyed. The men made daring mercy missions into the hills carrying supplies and organizing rest camps for the refugees on route; their womenfolk meanwhile set up emergency hospitals and welfare centres for those who reached safety.

Mrs J. Mills was living in Shillong, where her husband was now Advisor to the Governor, when the first refugee groups arrived. They were given food, clothes, blankets and sent down to Calcutta on the narrow gauge trains that came back up loaded with men and ammunition. The second wave to arrive – mainly Anglo-Indians, Indians, Burmans – were 'in a very poor way'. The jungle tracks had become 'seas of mud due to the monsoonal rains and a lot of them had been cut off by floods and landslides and died on route'. The survivors were suffering 'from every kind of disease and half-starved'.

The women ran camps for them outside Shillong: 'We sat them in rows and doled out curry and rice.' But food soon ran short in the town; electricity and water supplies were often cut; ambulances charged up and down the hills; air-raid sirens sounded as Japanese planes flew over; more slit-trenches were dug. It was certainly a time of emergency: 'One was even allowed into Government House without hats, gloves or stockings' for the first time in British memory. Mrs Mills volunteered for cipher duties and, as she was pregnant, was allowed to work at home with a *chaprassis* on guard outside. When the siren went, he carried the heavy cipher boxes to a slit trench behind the bungalow and she followed with the keys on a chain round her neck.

Mrs Veronica Westmacott who, in the jollier past, had pranced about her tennis court in the headlamps' limelight, was also initiated into the mysteries of codes and ciphers. First, she had to sign the Official Secrets Act – a 'most dramatic occasion' with men sitting solemnly round a table saying 'I could be shot if I gave anything away'. The actual work – of decoding incoming signals or coding outgoing ones – was 'not at all difficult, especially if one had done crosswords'.

Anti-aircraft batteries were positioned all through the tea estates, while the tea gardens were used as casualty clearing stations. Their wards 'had a terrible smell for a long time afterwards – of literally rotting humanity.' The Westmacotts' estate was in a strategic area of Assam, and a high piece of its ground 'where wild turkeys used to do their courting dances in the Spring' was made into an airfield called Dinjan. From it, light planes flew off on reconnaissance and raids over enemy territory, while refugees, wounded soldiers and military VIP's landed on it. It was, incidentally, the airfield from which General Wingate, leader of the fabled Chindits, took off in a Mitchell on his last mission.

Mrs Westmacott, the only woman living on the airfield, was asked by the military authorities to wear uniform, but demurred because 'the men preferred to see me in pretty dresses'. As a preparation for her important and confidential work, she 'was taken to the rifle range and taught to shoot a rifle, which was too heavy for me except when resting on something. But I was told I could hit a man if he attacked me . . . Tommy guns were the most efficient, one of the numerous bullets would be sure to find its mark. However a revolver was the only weapon I had. I nearly shot my foot off, but I was told I could be very menacing. After hearing terrible tales of what the Japanese did to women, I was warned to keep the last bullet for myself.'

After she'd been working at the airfield for some months, the first Enigma machine was delivered. 'I had a sledge hammer in the office and I was instructed to smash it at once if there was any hint of enemy invasion.' An armed guard stood outside the door and an incinerator and cans of petrol were kept ready for the burning of cipher books if necessary. Once, when a Japanese advance was reported, 'I hid the silver down the well, but it made everyone so depressed that I put it on show again.' A boat equipped with arms and provisions was moored at a nearby river landing stage ready for emergency evacuation. It was all rather nerve-racking, especially when she was told that the enemy were in the habit of 'painting themselves green and quietly surrounding their objective without being noticed.'

Refugee camps were set up in the area and the roads leading to them became quagmires. 'There were gorgeous butterflies everywhere and [one refugee] told me they were feeding on the corpses along the Burma Road. If anyone was going to die they settled on him. He said it was the damn butterflies that made him determined to win through . . . Most of the refugees had endured incredible hardship, but when they reached a safe place they often lost their momentum and died.'

Allied planes dropped supplies for them: 'Doors were left off the planes and strong men strapped to the aircraft would kick out crates of chickens, pigs and eggs on parachutes . . . An American told me that one pig wouldn't go and they kicked it out backwards and it gave him such a look as it left the aircraft!' Tins of bully beef were thrown out too, but ran the risk of being destroyed by devout Hindu soldiers, for whom the cow, even in such guise, remained sacred.

Food was extremely short until the American Red Cross arrived bringing supplies and wearing practical uniforms for the job. 'The first time I saw seersucker', Veronica comments. A mobile canteen was started by WASB's (the Women's Auxiliary Service of Burma), and one soldier told Veronica admiringly that 'He'd never at any time in the Burma campaign been without a WASB between him and the enemy!' A WVS canteen was also started to serve the men on the airfields and gun batteries, and, during 1943 and 1944, a number of these became operational in the forward areas.

Lady Olive Crofton was one of several committed and energetic people who launched an appeal for more women from the safer Indian provinces to volunteer to work in these areas for three-monthly stretches. Volunteers had to be physically fit and prepared for 'real hard work, bad climates and heat'. To drive the point home, she described her own experience of running a WVS canteen along the strategically important Manipur Road. Arriving there in an army truck, she was allotted quarters in 'a kind of loose box, furnished with a chair, table, a charpoy and a hurricane lamp'. The earliest recruit on the scene, she had for company only 'Two toads that slept under the bed and rats that ate the toe of my only pair of shoes on the first night'. She shared the officers' mess basic fare of bully beef, bacon, beans and cheese fritters for breakfast.

The canteen was a mere 'hutment made of split and plaited bamboo with mud floors and a thatched roof' and it was divided into sections for the counter, a little shop, a billiard table and a small kitchen. Lady Crofton's day began at 7.30, when she 'literally kicked up the staff' who were sound asleep on the floor. Outside chores included topping up the water tank and the piles of wood for the stove; inside, kitchenware had to be cleaned, urns of tea brewed, stores ordered from the Supply Depot, huge batches of sandwiches cut, 'It was not easy, but compared to the men we were in clover.'

At unpredictable times, but most often in the evenings, any numbers of men (from around sixty up to seven or eight hundred) came crowding in. Men from road convoys, 'white with dust and with red streaming eyes . . . Men from the gunsites, isolated out there in the blue. They would be single emissaries sent in with little shopping lists from their detachments. They wanted cigarettes of course, airgraph forms, handkerchiefs and toothpaste.' At the end they asked hopefully for a pipe or torch batteries, 'which were seldom available'. The toughest and most war-weary were the jungle fighters: 'Green-clad men these, their camouflaged uniforms torn by bushes, some with heads shaved or stained with camouflage too and all armed with *kukris* as well as bayonets.'

At the end of her canteen stint, Lady Crofton got a lift up the Manipur Road to Kohima on the mail delivery truck, and it was then that she briefly saw the Deputy Commissioner's bungalow and the scarlet canna lilies glowing in the sunshine. The road south, she observed, was optimistically signposted 'To Tokyo and the Far East'. Olive Crofton and other volunteers in the forward areas did about as much for the war effort as it was possible for female civilians without special qualifications to do. The women who did more, who sometimes spent months in dangerous proximity to the battle areas, were of course those with medical training who staffed the emergency hospitals and casualty centres.

One of them was Miss Denise Dane, formerly of St George's Hospital, Bombay – which must have seemed almost a sinecure compared to the jungle hospital five miles from the Burmese frontier where she spent most of 1943 and 1944. She was 'one of the TANs' (Territorial Army Nursing Sisters) and the hospital to which one 'bumped along over jungle tracks in an army lorry' was just a cluster of huts and tents. Goats, hens and ducks that were kept for the kitchens foraged about in the surrounding mud; living quarters were, to say the least, 'primitive' and leaked in the rains. Miss Dane was acting matron of this frail establishment, with only three white nurses under her and a patient intake 'of up to two thousand'.

Among them were numbers of Chindits – pallid, exhausted, often desperately sick, or wounded, after fighting behind the Japanese lines – but heroes in the eyes of the rest. 'The most fearful disease we had to contend with was cerebral malaria which could strike a man down at noon and kill him by three in the afternoon.' 'Ordinary' malaria was bad enough and many died of it too because the hospital ran out of supplies of quinine when the Japanese conquered Indonesia, from where it was sent. Cholera was another scourge; sufferers were isolated in separate tents on intravenous drips, but the 'recovery rate wasn't high'.

In due course, American casualties began to arrive and they 'wouldn't allow black soldiers in beds next to white ones. The Indians didn't want to be near the blacks either – but I'll say this for the British Tommy, he didn't object to any skin colour'. In such difficult conditions the nurses began to suffer from jungle sores, lice and ringworm and when 'a Lady Chief arrived to inspect us, we all sat there scratching and the sight of us soon sent her away!' Continuously overworked, exhausted and itchy, Denise Dane gave little thought to the threat of a Japanese advance. 'We had orders to stay at our posts whatever happened. And that was that.'

Many nurses who served in the forward areas have similar stories of danger, discomfort, exhaustion, sheer staying-power and simple courage. And, in her book, *The Maturing Sun*, Angela Bolton vividly describes how the war went for her as a member of the Queen Alexandra's Royal Army Nursing Corps. She reached India just as the British were in retreat from Burma and had therefore gained consider-able experience of wartime nursing by the time she was posted to Assam in the autumn of 1943. Her hospital was at Gauhati, north of Shillong, and patients, British and Indian, were accommodated in wood and bamboo *bashas*. 'Some of the floors were of dried mud, others covered with woven matting; functional electric light bulbs hanging from the rafters and electrically-powered punkahs gave erratic witness to the presence of the twentieth century . . . But the *bhiste* made no concession to the modern world whatever. In dry weather he squatted in the sandy dust, scouring the tin plates and utensils with the earth around him before rinsing them scrupulously clean with water from a brass bowl.'

Gauhati was 'a bottleneck between mid-Assam and India' and therefore strategically vulnerable, especially when the Japanese launched their last big offensive. 'Sick and wounded soldiers and airmen from the Fourteenth Army poured into the wards . . . There was no question of separating surgical and medical cases. The soldier with his jaw shot away could still develop an attack of malaria, for there was a shortage of specially proofed mosquito nets and mepacrine tablets could be forgotten in the heat of battle.'

Among 'the unending turnover of patients' was a British soldier with a badly infected leg wound that had proved resistant to sulfa drugs, so he faced an amputation. Angela and her colleagues were summoned to the side ward where he lay. 'Major Niblock and Joan Inman [a nurse] were there, dressed as for an operation in gauze masks, sterile gowns and rubber gloves. The major was drawing some yellow liquid into a large syringe. He held it up to the light saying, "This is the new drug which has just arrived. It is called penicillin and we are going to try it out on this patient." After carefully cleaning the skin he injected the drug into a muscle. When we returned three hours later to look at the leg, Major Niblock was saying as he gave the second injection, "I do believe it looks a little cleaner".' The infection receded, the soldier kept his leg and the 'miracle drug', though still 'precious as gold' proved its worth in many of the forward area hospitals during the latter stages of the war.

It was typical of this campaign for infections and tropical diseases to kill more men than bombs or bullets and, in the 'unhealthy month of July' Gauhati hospital was stricken with a cholera epidemic. After watching 'with a morbid fascination the small curved comma-bacillus wriggling about under the microscope', Angela Bolton was sent to the 'large isolation *basha* where the beds were dotted about the room to make access to the bedside easy for the sweepers. Each patient lay on a wooden bedframe, whose coir-rope supports held the emaciated bodies as in a hammock. Under each bed stood a large bowl to catch the continual gushes of "rice-water" motions which produced dehydration in the victim. The mosquito nets reached to the floor to prevent the entry of flies . . . From all around came the groans of patients suffering from painful cramps in the muscles of the arms, legs and abdomen, mingled with the sounds of vomiting and intense purging. Patiently the little band of carefully instructed sweepers went about their horrid task of emptying and renewing bowls. So must the wards of Scutari have looked to the Crimean nurses.'

The strain on all the medical staff was prolonged and unrelenting and they yearned for the respite of short leaves in Darjeeling or Calcutta. The latter city had grown quite accustomed to influxes of troops and refugees by this time and its Firpo's Restaurant – renowned for its band and its servings of icecream with hot chocolate sauce – seemed like paradise after months of wartime jungli living. Joyce Taylor, a nurse attached to the Air Force Nursing Service Reserve, remembers enjoying Firpo's icecream in 1944 and going on to the cinema 'where you always sat on your coat because of the bugs'. No shortage of escorts for an evening out in a city where white women were 'at a premium'; at dances, 'the chaps were waiting like hawks at a fence' and she was once approached for the same dance by 'an entire air-crew just back from Burma'.

She helped to open a new hospital for RAF personnel in Calcutta, in a dirty old building that 'had stood empty for ages' and lacked every medical requirement. Then she was posted to Cawnpore and to Chittagong and, having to cope with raw recruits as well as 'hardened old campaigners out of Burma', soon became quite 'a tough old biddy' herself. In Cawnpore, soldiers were sent on long route marches in the fierce noonday sun, and 'I remember stringing up about forty bodies wrapped in wet sheets and with lumps of ice on their chests' who'd been felled by heatstroke. In Chittagong, she was accommodated in a 'nice little *basha*' with a canvas bath and a canvas bucket, camp bed and stool – though there were layers of red dust over everything.

The Air Ministry decreed that the nurses should wear white dresses, which was ridiculous in all that heat and dust. 'After a few washes in the village ponds the dresses were khaki anyway', while stockings caused prickly heat. So they usually wore khaki bush jackets and trousers that were much more sensible when you were always on the move. For that was the life; never settled anywhere for long before orders came to pack up your kitbag and bedroll with 'all your worldly goods – tin plate, mug, irons for eating, folded mosquito net and as many "bunnies" [sanitary towels] as you could squeeze in'.

But keeping on the move was often preferable to being cooped up in the same hospital for too long – or so Angela

Bolton decided when she put in for a transfer to the River
Steamer Unit. The unit consisted of eight paddle steamers,
marked with large red crosses to discourage enemy bombing and propelled by still-reliable engines made on Clyde-
side in the nineteenth century. The vessels conveyed
patients from the Gauhati hospital on a thirty-six-hour
voyage down the Brahmaputra River to Sirajganj for
onward transport by train to Dacca or Calcutta.

A medical officer was in command of each, with two QA
nurses, orderlies, and a 'crew that seemed to consist of
representatives of every nation east of Suez. The ships'
masters were always Muslims from Chittagong . . . With
their long flowing white beards they looked like Old
Testament prophets, but their black embroidered waist-
coats and red fez hats added a swashbuckling element to
their appearance.' In the prow of each ship 'stood a
member of the crew with a graduated pole, whose business
it was to measure the depth of the water, particularly when
the channel was narrow. He shouted, or rather intoned, the
measurements in a rhythmic manner, rather like a religious
chant, and the mournful dirge accompanied our progress
by day and night. The master was frequently to be seen
aloft surveying his kingdom, his long white beard streaming in the wind, his hawk's eye alert for signs of sandbanks
ahead.'

During the hot weather and monsoon season of 1944,
there were so many patients that Sister Bolton often worked
in the hospital wards all day and then went off on the
steamer at 6 p.m., remaining on duty for the entire voyage.
The steamers too were crowded. On one trip, 'We carried
ten gunners from Assam and sixty Chindits with two very
ill officers. They filled every available space, many of them
lying wearily on their straw mattresses gazing at the
passing scenery, only too glad to be in an area where they
were safe from sudden death. Most of them looked like
skeletons as a result of dysentary, malaria and general
privation. It was pathetic to see these bundles of skin and

bone trying to eat the good meals provided – chicken broth and canned pears being the favourites. They would ask for a generous helping, start to eat avidly, then put the plate down with regret, their stomachs not able to cope with anything stronger than milk and eggs.'

But for Angela there was always the return trips to look forward to when she, now the only Westerner on board, 'decided to adapt myself to the Indian way of life'. She wore a sari, listened to Indian music, even tried dancing to it, learned to enjoy South Indian curries and found 'the evenings on the foredecks delightful. They were spent listening to stories of Hindu gods and goddesses . . . Later we would fall silent, gazing riverwards at the sampans silhouetted against a primrose sky. The village huts, like nests at the foot of mop-headed palms, the thick jungle coming down to the water's edge, the rocky islands in midstream were all transformed by the rays of the setting sun which, during the monsoon season, had that rare quality of changing and heightening the colours of land and water.'

For many months Sister Bolton was a regular member of the medical team who sailed up and down the Brahmaputra on mercy missions that sometimes extended as far as Dacca in East Bengal. There, when the patients had been taken off to the British General Hospital, she and her companions went shopping in the bazaar, swimming in the Club pool and, in the evenings, Mr McKertich, a jovial Scottish jute manager, sometimes invited them to his large house beside the river. He always provided 'opulent meals organized by his excellent *khitmagar* (butler)', and then whirled his guests downstream in his private launch to the Club where plenty of whisky flowed to the music of the bagpipes.

Arriving at Dacca on a later date in May 1945, 'Mr McKertich came on board followed by his *khitmagar* who was carrying a heavy wireless . . . In the evening as we all gathered together on deck, we were rewarded by the sound of a newsreader's voice announcing that the war in Europe was over at last.' The following day they again gathered round the wireless '. . . to hear the King's speech at 1.30 p.m. and Winston Churchill's address to the nation at 7.30 p.m. We had lunch on deck, rather guiltily drinking a bottle of champagne from the Red Cross stores . . .'

For those fighting the Japanese the war was not yet over of course, but it was now further removed from the Indian frontiers and, as fewer patients arrived at the Gauhati hospital, Angela Bolton's period of riverine nursing drew to a close. Among the many sick men carried on the old paddle-steamers had been casualties from the heavy fighting that occurred in and around Kohima during the spring of 1944 when a small British garrison held out for three weeks against a Japanese division.

That white bungalow on the hill where Mrs Mills once lived, where the men of the Assam Rifles ceremoniously lowered the Union Jack at every peaceful sunset, became a battleground. Trenches were dug on the tennis court where the planters used to play and much blood ran where the scarlet cannas had once bloomed. Lady Crofton, who saw them in their last flowering, flew low over Kohima a few months after the battle and recorded: 'Only the shape of spurs made the place recognizable now. Where the lovely little station had stood such a short time before was a blasted ridge, bare but for a few blackened stumps and, on one side of it, a space had been cleared and was filled with rows of little wooden crosses.'

Many countries of the world were never the same again after the second world war, and India was certainly one of them. The period that followed its end and the granting of Independence in 1947 saw more violence and bloodshed within its boundaries than had occurred during the war itself. For the British who remained there was no return to the comparative security of the prewar Raj and that short postwar era was quite different and, in many ways, less pleasant for them than what had gone before. And so it came about that the great majority of women who feature in this chapter because they were living and working in India during the war had left the country, usually forever, within three years of its conclusion.

But many of the British women who lived in India for any length of time, either then or in the earlier decades of the century, never forgot their experiences of it. Their retrospective books, memoirs and recordings reveal an extraordinary degree of wistful nostalgia and abiding affection for the country where they often claim to have spent some of their happiest years. They were younger then of course, and it is the passing of the orderly securities of India ruled by the British that they regret. Their recollections of that vanished land are incomplete, selective, flawed, for they remember what they want to remember, what they were brought up to remember. But of such stuff history is always made and it does not make their contribution to it any less valid.

In conclusion then, I hope this picture of British women's lives in India will finally dispel the notion that their sole occupations were playing bridge and tennis, gossiping at the club and flirting at the hill station. That was, of course, the life for some, and it has been exhaustively chronicled elsewhere, particularly in fiction. This record is as near factual as such records can be, and will, I trust, add a little more weight and lustre to 'the dust in the balance'.

Sources

PERSONAL INTERVIEWS AND CORRESPONDENCE: PRIVATELY HELD MATERIAL

Anderson, J.
Clayton, E.
Crawford, D.
Dane, D.
Davidson, S.
Frater, M.
Frost, P.
Godfrey, M.
James, I.
Kennedy, M.
King-Martin, J.
Le Mesurier, M.
Macdonald, B.
Middleton, D.
Morris, E.

Morrison, M.
Patterson, J.
Portal, I.
Rasmussen, J.
Ricardo, M.
Roseveare, R.
Short, R.
Straus, G.
Swayne-Thomas, A.
Sykes, M.
Taylor, J.
Wickham, J.
Wright, J.
Wright, M.

PRIVATE PAPERS IN PUBLIC COLLECTIONS
Centre of South Asian Studies

Anderson, J.
Battye, D.
Bayley, B.
Bayley, V.
Bourne, H.
Champion, H.

Clough, M.
Crofton, O.
Crookshank, I.
Cunliffe-Parsons, M.
Dench, M.
Farquarson, E.

Hall, M.
Hammersley-Smith, M.
Henderson, C.
Lacey, P.
Meiklejohn, F.
Mills, J.
Mullan, K.
Portal, I.

Ravenscroft, M.
Ross, E.
Stokes, A.
Stuart, H.
Sykes, M.
Turner, D.
Tyler, H.

India Office Library

Diamond, B.
Dixon, E.
Fitzroy, Y.
Hamilton, O.
Lee, A.
Norie, G.
Roberts, R.
Rowe, D.
Thomson, C.

Ussher, M.
Vernede, N.
Walsh, M.
Westmacott, V.
Wilkins, H.
Williamson, M.
Wilson, E.
Wyld, F.

Imperial War Museum

Davidson, S.

BIBLIOGRAPHY

Balfour, M. and Young, R.: *The Work of Medical Women in India*, Oxford University Press, 1929.

Baylis, A.: *And Then Garwhal*, BACSA, 1981.

Bolton, A.: *The Maturing Sun*, Headline Book Publishing PLC, 1988.

Butler, I. (ed): *Countess Reading, The Viceroy's Wife*, Hodder & Stoughton Ltd, 1969.

Chitty, J. (ed): *Anna Chitty: Musings of a Memsahib, 1921–33*, Belhaven, 1988.

Coelho, D.: *Orchids and Algebra*, private printing, 1986.

Cousins, J. and M.: *We Two Together*, Ganesh & Co, Madras, 1950.

Fitzroy, Y.: *Courts and Camps in India*, Methuen & Co Ltd, 1926.

Godden, R.: *Bengal Journey*, Longman, 1945.

Hinkson, P.: *Indian Harvest*, William Collins, Sons & Co Ltd, 1941.

Macdonald, B.: *India: Sunshine and Shadow*, BACSA, 1988.

Mayo, K.: *Mother India*, Jonathan Cape Ltd, 1927.

Nanda, B.: contribution in *Indian Women: From Purdah to Modernity* (Nehru Memorial Museum & Library), Vikas, 1976.

Roseveare, R.: *Community of St Stephen 1886–1986*, private printing, 1986.

Starr, L.: *The Colonel's Lady*, G. Bell & Son, 1937.

Watney, G. G. and Lloyd, Mrs H.: *India for the Motorist*, Car Illustrated, 1913.

Wilkins, Dr E. G.: *By Hands, Bullocks and Prayers*, private printing, 1987.

Wilson, Clarke D.: *Doctor Ida*, Vellore Christian Medical Board, 1959.

Wright, M.: *Under Malabar Hill*, BACSA, 1988.

Index